SELF-HYPNOSIS

YOUR GOLDEN KEY TO SELF-IMPROVEMENT AND SELF-HEALING

Norbert W. Bakas, PhD, DNGH

Self-Hypnosis
Your Golden Key to Self-Improvement and Self-Healing

Copyright © 2010 by Norbert W. Bakas, PhD, DNGH

ISBN 1452894027
EAN-13 9781452894027

All rights reserved. No part of this book may be reproduced or transmitted in any form or by any means without written permission of the author.

This book contains advice and information relating to health care. It is not intended to replace medical advice and should be used to supplement rather than replace regular care by your doctor. It is recommended that you seek your physician's advice before embarking on any medical program or treatment.

Acknowledgments

Acknowledgement is a word that is far too inadequate to describe my gratitude and indebtedness to my mentor and friend, Dr. John C. Hughes. Dr. Hughes is a highly esteemed research writer, whose many books deserve top space in the library of every hypnotist. Without his encouragement, sage advice, editing, comments, and actively steering the manuscript throughout the pre-publishing processes, this book would never have been published.

Norbert Bakas, PhD, DNGH

Foreword

Norbert Bakas, the author of this practical book on self-hypnosis, is recognized for his expertise in the field of hypnotism. In sharing his knowledge of self-hypnosis he has made available to others the benefit of his skill, philosophy and technique.

This practical book on self-hypnosis was written by a remarkable man who has been teaching and practicing hypnosis for over sixty-seven years. (At the time of this writing, Norbert Bakas is 87 and still active in hypnosis.) Private Bakas entered the Army serving throughout World War II and participated in the battle of Iwo Jima. After the war he remained in the Active Army Reserve and through an interservice transfer became a full-time member of the Air National Guard. After 40 years of military service, Norbert retired in 1983 as a Lieutenant Colonel. He got involved with hypnosis shortly after his enlistment in the Army and performed educational lecture-demonstrations of hypnotism, and practiced hypnotherapy in the evenings. Awarded a PhD from LaSalle University in 1995, he taught over 100 45-hour courses in self-hypnosis at Community College of Allegheny in Pittsburgh, Pennsylvania.

When I first met Norbert at the National Guild of Hypnotists Convention in Nashua, New Hampshire fifteen years ago, we talked about the emerging field of hypnotism. What makes this meeting memorable was a demonstration of self-hypnosis by Norbert that astounded me. He said with self-hypnosis he could control the circulation of blood in his body. After removing his suit coat, Norbert rolled up his shirt sleeve and after a brief reverie of concentration, his left arm and hand became intensely red. He then said that he would reverse the flow of blood in his arm. In a matter of moments his left arm and hand went from a hyperemic crimson red to chalk white.

The following day, while my wife and I were waiting to be seated in a restaurant, I noticed Norbert and his wife behind us. After mutual introductions of our wives, I asked him to repeat the demonstration of the previous evening for the benefit of my wife. He obliged me with the same startling results.

Norbert then told us about a time when he made use of self-hypnosis in an emergency. "After teaching a very strenuous class in water safety, I returned home at about 11:00 PM physically exhausted. As I was nearing the back entrance to my house my legs buckled and collapsed and I was impaled on a ¾-inch angle-iron post next to my back sidewalk. I immediately applied the suggestion that I did not feel a thing (I didn't) and then suggested that there would be no bleeding. When I pulled my leg off the post it didn't bleed. The wound was about 1 to 1½ inches deep. I asked my wife to get a bandage, and she insisted that we go to the hospital. The ER doctor said that it was a serious wound and asked me about the pain. My response was, 'You do the sewing, doctor, and I'll take care of the pain.' He put in 40 stitches and said I would have a terrible scar. There is no scar."

The contents of this information-packed book are organized under fifteen headings. The book opens with a concise explanation about hypnosis and how the subconscious mind works. The second chapter shows how hypnotism evolved and provides historical perspectives by relating the contributions of hypnotism's most recognized proponents. The third chapter is an excellent overview of the mind. Chapter four describes the mind-body connection and its importance to health. Chapter five introduces the reader to Emile Coué, who in the 1920s introduced a method of psychotherapy, healing, and self-improvement, based on autosuggestion or self-hypnosis. Coué is remembered for his formula for curing by autosuggestion: "Every day, in every way, I am getting better and better." Chapter six covers the author's formula (or technique) for successful self-hypnosis. Chapter seven emphasizes the importance of perseverance or commitment in achieving a successful outcome. Chapter eight describes the important role of relaxation in our lives and well-being. Chapter nine is about how to use imagery and imagination in self-hypnosis. Chapter ten is about the power of belief and its role in successful self-hypnosis. Chapter eleven explains the important role of suggestion in self-hypnosis. Chapter 12 gives details on the use of an audio recorder as an aid to the induction of self-hypnosis. Chapter 13 describes alternative approaches to achieve self-hypnosis. In Chapter 14 the reader learns to take sensible precautions to avoid potential problems. The concluding chapter is entitled "Threshold of a New Era" and is devoted to the future of self-hypnosis as a tool for self-improvement and self-healing.

Every once in a while you read something that makes what you already know wake up and come alive once more. *Self-Hypnosis: Your Golden Key to Self-Improvement and Self-Healing* is such a book. It is jargon-free and clearly written. Beginners and old hands alike will find this book a joy to read and extremely valuable.

John C. Hughes, D.C., DNGH
Author of *The Illustrated History of Hypnotism*

Table of Contents

CHAPTER 1	*The Case for Hypnosis*	1
CHAPTER 2	*Alternative Medicine and Hypnosis*	11
CHAPTER 3	*Your Mind in Hypnosis*	21
CHAPTER 4	*Mind-Body Connection*	31
CHAPTER 5	*Mastery of Self-Hypnosis*	43
CHAPTER 6	*My Formula for Successful Self-Hypnosis*	53
CHAPTER 7	*Commitment*	59
CHAPTER 8	*Relaxation*	65
CHAPTER 9	*Imagery and Imagination*	71
CHAPTER 10	*Belief*	77
CHAPTER 11	*Suggestions*	85
CHAPTER 12	*The Indispensable Audio CD Recorder*	93
CHAPTER 13	*Other Routes to Self-Hypnosis*	101
CHAPTER 14	*Sensible Precautions*	105
CHAPTER 15	*Threshold of a New Era*	113
BIBLIOGRAPHY		117

CHAPTER 1
The Case for Hypnosis

"Seek not abroad, turn back into thy self, for in the inner man dwells the truth." ~ St. Augustine (A.D. 400)

All of us, at one time or another, have wished that we had a little black box and that by pushing buttons we could achieve a state of relaxation, eliminate stress, or abolish destructive habits. We also wish that we could push a button that would transfer our focus from negative thinking into positive and productive ideas. We would like the power to improve our physical prowess, accelerating our healing processes and prevent illness.

Good news! Rather than wishing, we can realize we DO possess that almost magical control box—in fact, we are born with it. To be more precise, the control box IS your subconscious mind, and learning how to communicate with it can become an exciting and rewarding challenge. One must realize, however, that this communication is a two-way circuit which, when implanting the desired effect into one's mind, can produce multiple improvements and the awakening of our many latent endowments.

Yoga or meditation is often accepted as a means of communication with one's subconscious mind. These methods are related to hypnosis to some degree, depending upon the specific nature of the subject matter.

Some yoga disciplines require years of dedicated effort to master. However, by employing hypnosis, an individual may hasten the process of physical and mental relaxation and thereby facilitate an access into the inner subconscious mind. This process allows both the amassing of valuable information and the ability to draw from that reserve whenever it is needed.

Students interested in the study of hypnosis commonly ask, "I've read many books on the subject and, while I have followed their instructions, it just doesn't seem to work for me. What am I doing wrong?"

A multitude of books have been written on the subject of hypnotism and self-hypnosis by learned and experienced hypnotists. Other authors approaching the subject write beautifully but without the slightest concept of either hypnotism or hypnotherapy.

As a hypnotist, I am familiar with the multiple functions attributed to the human mind, and with the impediments that contribute to the formation of fears, phobias, and other mental disorders. Having worked with over 75,000 clients in the past sixty-seven years, I have found many applications of hypnosis that can benefit individuals possessing psychosomatic conditions. I have learned to assist the client to apply induced positive attitudes, thereby promoting rapid healing and the reduction of distress relative to other ailments.

There have been many theories postulated to explain changes in emotions and attitudes within one's mental framework. Some authorities believe that all our actions are induced by chemical changes and interactions. Others lean toward the view that the primary influence on our behavior is electrical in nature; while still others believe that we act and feel because of a spiritual or divine power.

Consider the enigma of the mind as compared to magnetism, electricity, or even the wind. How can one adequately describe these intangible energies? With modern technology we now have the knowledge to generate electricity economically and to effectively utilize it, along with its magnetic applications. We have harnessed the power of wind for thousands of years, with windmills and sailing ships. But we know very little of the natural generation of these forces, how to control them, or even a proper manner to describe them.

Professionally, I have observed and experienced thousands of cases where the power of mind control, associated with positive attitudes, has vastly improved the quality of human life. I have seen it dramatically enhance athletic abilities and contribute immeasurably toward rapid healing, helping to eliminate many existing medical problems. The power of that imaginary black box is entrenched within each of us and positive results can be expected, but only if we are willing to learn and practice the principles of self-hypnosis. The results obtainable by the proper utilization of self-hypnosis are seemingly limitless. ***Think about it!***

William C. Gibson explained:

The best that I can do is to abstractly theorize that since all mental activity apparently is in the form of electro-chemical impulses, a condition of self-hypnosis somehow closes a "high-voltage" direct circuit between the conscious and the subconscious portions of the mind with the inclusion of a "static-eliminator" in the circuit to shut off random interference. This clear, powerful and direct connection permits an unimpeded flow of impulses (i.e. thoughts, instructions, memories, etc.) back and forth within the mind.

Under normal conditions, the flow seems to be circuitous through many small and often short circuited networks of tiny and uncertain connections. In any event, the ability to create and direct self-hypnosis has been found to be inherent within every human mind, although HOW or WHY it functions does remain open to question. WHAT it does is demonstrable.

For some people, it has been found that the condition can be achieved promptly and easily. For others, several attempts may be required and full success may be more gradual in its achievement. Generally, any person who can concentrate a significant portion of his conscious attention intently upon some very simple instructions and upon following these instructions can achieve this desirable and beneficial condition.[1]

At all times one should maintain an attitude of reality at any level of expectations. Take for example a high jumper, who could improve his or her performance by removing whatever inhibitions may be hindering their efforts. The result would be that they would very likely exceed their own previous records. However, it would be inappropriate to aspire to jumping higher than attainable. Projected results must stay within the province of rational expectations and also within a flexible time period.

"How-To" books are published covering almost every conceivable subject, ranging from practical guides on the wiring of a telephone, or furniture repair, to manuals relating to various aspects of ethereal achievements. Too often, however, a reader's efforts are met by disappointment and frustration.

We are a nation of wanting things done yesterday. We expect immediate results and are perhaps unwilling to persevere with patience on whatever subject we pursue. The subconscious mind must be appeased before it renders whatever favors it deems appropriate to grant.

In the teaching of self-hypnosis, many hypnotherapists will advocate that an aspirant first experience a state of hypnosis by being hypnotized by a qualified hypnotist. Thus the individual will more readily recognize the feeling associated with the trance state and develop a reference point for his feelings while in a hypnotic state.

Anyone could experience self-hypnosis without fully realizing what it was, or its true potential, and consequently relinquish their attempts in the mistaken belief that they were unsuccessful. Some people have disclosed that they practiced yoga and meditation and have experienced similar states of relaxation or mental control yet had never experienced that identical feeling with self-hypnosis.

We should be aware of what we are seeking, then find it and recognize what it is before utilizing it for a desired purpose. Hypnosis and self-hypnosis are a result of self-expectancy, and therefore it is essential that one should understand specifically what they can expect to both feel and experience in the state of self-hypnosis.

Whenever engaging in hypnosis or a state of self-hypnosis, one is:

In complete control of one's state of mind

Aware of what the hypnotist or recording is saying

Always conscious

In a state of concentrated attention

Able to terminate the trance state at will

Since your mind accepts behavioral changes automatically, self-hypnosis tends to cause improvements to become more permanent because of the pleasure derived from the "better way." This would be much like reverting to an old mechanical adding machine following the usage of an exciting new calculator. Neither would one wish to return to the outdated typewriter of yesteryear after being exposed to a computer word processing program. We normally prefer working by the easiest, simplest, and most improved manner possible.

All hypnosis is basically self-hypnosis. Nearly anyone can hypnotize themselves when they know how it is accomplished. Self-hypnosis can influence the subconscious mind positively, but first you must change your way of thinking.

In 1922 C. Harry Brooks wrote:

Every idea which enters the mind, if it is accepted by the Unconscious, is transformed by it into a reality and forms henceforth a permanent element in our life. This is the process called "Spontaneous Autosuggestion." It is a law by which all our minds are working daily.

The reader will see from the examples cited and from others which he will constantly meet that the thoughts we think determine not only our mental states, our sentiments and emotions, but the delicate actions and adjustments of our physical bodies. Trembling, palpitation, stammering, blushing—not to speak of the pathological states which occur in neurosis—are due to modifications and changes in the blood-flow, in muscular action and in the working of the vital organs. These changes are not voluntary and conscious ones, they are determined by the Unconscious and come to us often with a shock of surprise.

It must be evident that if we fill our conscious minds with ideas of health, joy, goodness, efficiency, and can ensure their acceptance by the Unconscious, these ideas too will become realities, capable of lifting us on to a new plane of being. The difficulty which has hitherto so frequently brought these hopes to naught is that of ensuring acceptance.

To sum up, the whole process of Autosuggestion consists of two steps: (1) The acceptance of an idea. (2) Its transformation into a reality. Both these operations are performed by the Unconscious. Whether the idea is originated in the mind of the subject or is presented from without by the agency of another person is a matter of indifference. In both cases it undergoes the same process: it is submitted to the Unconscious, accepted or rejected, and so either realized or ignored. Thus the distinction between Autosuggestion and Hetero-suggestion is seen to be both arbitrary and superficial. In essentials, all suggestion is Autosuggestion. The only distinction we need to make is between Spontaneous Autosuggestion, which takes place independently of our will and choice, and induced Autosuggestion, in which we consciously select the ideas we wish to realize and purposely convey them to the Unconscious.[2]

Through the benefits of self-hypnosis, we can learn to relax the body and mind, thereby causing ourselves to respond more readily to positive suggestions. All sensible goals that we seek are realistically achieved through this means.

Medical research has indicated that 76% to 84% of illnesses has its origin in the mind and are referred to as psychosomatic illnesses. It must be remembered that self-hypnosis becomes beneficial and effective when it receives constructive suggestions to program the mind. **In short, what your mind has caused, your mind can cure.**

Autosuggestion influences the mind by your own positive (or negative) thinking. Self-healing can be accomplished through your acceptance and application of positive self-suggestion.

In self-hypnosis, we are establishing a communication circuit between the conscious and subconscious mind.

There are various terms used for self-hypnosis, including:
1. Self-Hypnosis

Auto-Suggestion

Auto-Conditioning

Self-Suggestion

Auto-Hypnosis

Huna

Couéism

Meditation

To paraphrase—If it walks like a duck, quacks like a duck, looks like a duck—then it is a duck. If it sounds like self-hypnosis, works like self-hypnosis, and achieves the results of self-hypnosis, then it is **SELF-HYPNOSIS.**

References

1. William C. Gibson, *Therapeutic Self-Hypnosis* (New York, NY: Caravelle Books Inc., 1967), pp. 36-37.
2. Harry C. Brooks, *The Practice of Autosuggestion* (New York, NY: Dodd, Mead & Co., 1922), pp. 54-56.

Other readings

Salter, Andrew. *What is Hypnosis.* New York, NY: Farrar, Straus & Co., 1944.

Kirtley, Christine. *Consumer Guide to Hypnosis.* Merrimack, NH: National Guild of Hypnotists, 1991.

Straus, Roger A. *Creative Self-Hypnosis.* New York, NY: Prentice Hall Press, 1989.

Hariman, Jusuf. *How to use the Power of Self-Hypnosis.* Wellingborough, Northamptonshire, UK: Thorson's Publishers Limited, 1981.

CHAPTER 2
Alternative Medicine and Hypnosis

"The most high hath created medicines out of the earth, and a wise man will not abhor them." ~Ecclesiastes 38:4

The trance state had been known from the earliest beginnings of the human race. It is the bedrock of shamanism in all its variations among primitive peoples, from Siberia to South America, from Australia to West Africa. The shaman induces himself into an autohypnotic trance state through techniques that are extremely similar everywhere. This has led several scholars to propose that such techniques are the strongest argument in support of the theory that all peoples have sprung from a common ancestry. In this self-hypnotic trance, the shaman enters into the realm of the subconscious, in which his imaging faculties have full play. He returns to waking consciousness to predict the future, to perform healings, to cast spells and counter-spells.

All of this, however, is far removed from any normalized corpus of doctrine and application. While a variety of clearly hypnotic methods of inducing trance were known to all the civilizations of antiquity, there is no evidence that a form of clinical hypnosis was anywhere established as a separate discipline with accepted modes of procedure. The closest approach to this was in the *Asklepeia* sleep temples that appeared in the final, Hellenistic phase of the ancient Greek civilization. These seem to have derived from models in late Pharaonic Egypt, which in turn were probably elaborated from more individualized forms of treatment that had persisted through close to two thousand years.

The difficulty in antiquity, which carried through into the Middle Ages and the early modern period, was that there was neither an adequate understanding of the subconscious or of the power of suggestion, nor any general body of doctrine into which the induction of the trance state and its effects could be fitted. Countless healers and practitioners of healing magic employed the trance state, benignly or otherwise, but each did so in their own way. No one tried to write an exposition or instructions (at least none have survived or come to modern knowledge) that others could follow and replicate their results.

Franz Anton Mesmer (1734-1815) virtually had to create both the discipline of animal magnetism--the precursor of modern hypnotism--and its doctrinal context. The culture of the eighteenth century enlightenment, of which he was a product, provided him with the necessary intellectual framework, which had never previously existed on such a scale.

Mesmer, however, was degraded and denounced by the French Medical Society who requested a royal commission to investigate his magnetism claims and procedures. Although the committee reviewed numerous documented cases of patients who were cured by Mesmer's unorthodox treatment; the investigative committee could not find the existence of Mesmer's postulated "animal magnetic fluid" and denounced Mesmer as a charlatan by stating that animal magnetic fluid does not exist and therefore cannot be useful. The so called "cures", they concluded, were brought about by the patient's imagination.

Until recently only a few medical doctors had the fortitude to employ hypnosis in their respective practices. These early pioneers of hypnosis were often ostracized, ridiculed, and unrecognized by their fellow medical practitioners. They were not permitted to perform this beneficial service for their patients in hospitals.

Dr. John Elliotson (1791-1868), who introduced the stethoscope in England (soon after Laennec's invention of it in France) was criticized and forbidden to talk or write about his knowledge of hypnotism. For thirteen years, John Elliotson published a newsletter entitled *ZOIST* in which he advocated and extolled the medical benefits of hypnosis.

Later, in the United States, Dr. Milton Erickson (1901-1980) encountered the same resistance from colleagues and hospitals alike in his fervent belief of the therapeutic value of hypnotism within the framework of the medical profession. In the decade of the 1950s Erickson became a nationally known figure, featured in the news media and consulted by famous athletes, the U.S. military, and the airline industry for improved performance by both individuals and groups. Even though the emphasis was still mainly on the psychology involved, and his masterly application of it through his innovative techniques, the fact that hypnotism was the most important of them was finally getting across to the public and to some portion of the medical profession. A giant step forward to greater acceptance of hypnotherapy was the founding in 1957, largely by Erickson's initiative, of the American Society of Clinical Hypnosis, with him as its first president and first editor of its Journal. He was the president for two years, and editor for ten years.

Official approval of hypnosis as a valid therapeutic modality was belated. It is interesting to note that the British Medical Association gave sanction for the use of hypnosis as an adjunct to medical treatment in 1954. The American Medical Association followed Britain's acceptance by announcing their approval in 1958.

The editors of *Alternative Medicine* have described 43 alternative therapies with information gathered from 350 leading-edge physicians who explain their treatments. Many of the methods require physical manipulation, the use of prescription drugs, herbs, etc., but the editors avoid referring to the mind-body connection which we associate with hypnosis. Therefore, we shall bypass these speculative methods.

Alternate therapies that are more closely associated with hypnosis include the following:

AYURVEDIC MEDICINE: The "science of life" has been in practice for over 5000 years in India. It combines natural therapies with a highly personalized approach in the treatment of disease. Ayurvedic medicine places equal emphasis on body, mind, and spirit, and strives to restore the innate harmony of the individual. [1]

BIOFEEDBACK TRAINING: Biofeedback teaches a person how to change and control his or her body's vital functions through the use of simple electronic devices. Biofeedback is particularly useful for learning to reduce stress, eliminate headaches, control asthmatic attacks, recondition injured muscles, and relieve pain.[2]

GUIDED IMAGERY: Guided imagery uses the power of the mind to evoke a positive physical response. Guided imagery can reduce stress and slow heart rate, stimulate the immune system, and reduce pain. As part of the rapidly emerging field of mind-body medicine, guided imagery is being used in various medical settings, and, when properly taught can also serve as a highly effective form of self-cure.[3] Guided imagery is a branch of hypnotism, since knowledgeable hypnotists have been using imagery for over 200 years. All qualified hypnotists are well versed in guided imagery techniques. Unfortunately not all guided imagery practitioners are trained in hypnosis.

MEDITATION: Meditation is a safe and simple way to balance a person's physical, emotional, and mental states. It is easily learned and has been used as an aid in treating stress and in pain management. It has also been employed as part of an overall treatment for other conditions, including hypertension and heart disease.[4]

MIND-BODY MEDICINE: This growing field may soon revolutionize modern health care. Recognizing the profound interconnection of mind and body, the body's innate healing capabilities, and the role of self-responsibility in the healing process, mind-body medicine utilizes a wide range of modalities, including biofeedback, imagery, hypnotherapy, meditation, and yoga.[5]

YOGA: Yoga is among the oldest-known systems of health practiced in the world today, and research into yoga practices has had a strong impact on the fields of stress reduction, mind-body medicine, and energy medicine. The physical postures, breathing exercises, and meditation practices of yoga have been proven to reduce stress, lower blood pressure, regulate heart rate, and even retard the aging process.[6]

HYPNOTHERAPY: Hypnotherapy is used to manage numerous medical and psychological problems. Hypnotic techniques can help a person stop smoking, overcome alcohol and substance abuse, and reduce overeating. Hypnotherapy is also effective in treating stress, sleep disorders, and mental health problems such as anxiety, fear, phobias, and depression.[7]

AUTOGENIC THERAPY (AT): AT is a highly systematized series of attention-focusing exercises designed to generate a state of mind and body relaxation. The training is the foundation for Autogenic Therapy, a process especially applicable to psychosomatic disorders. Autogenics is a kind of self-hypnosis, and is used to gain deep relaxation and enhance one's recuperative and self-healing powers. "Autogenic" means self-generated. AT's purpose is to give trainees the skills to put themselves in a relaxed state without depending on a trainer or guide. This state, akin to hypnosis or meditation, allows the body to release its own stress, muscle tension, and neuromuscular memories—the body's subconscious recollection of previous physical and emotional traumas. This relaxation and release frees the body to return to a homeostasis, or equilibrium.[8]

PAST LIFE THERAPY (PLT): PLT is the accessing of information or images from possible former lifetimes, usually through hypnotic regression or some form of an altered state of consciousness, for therapeutic purposes. Past Life Therapy differs from Past Life Regression in the use and meaning of the past life information.

Past life regression is a general term for probing the unconscious mind to retrieve historical memories or information from childhood or previous lives. The late Helen Wambaugh conducted thousands of past life regressions to collect historical data, past and future, to investigate the theory of reincarnation. Her group regression events were done for research and personal experience, not therapy. Subjects had no expectation of follow-up counseling to help them understand and deal with the information.

Past life therapy explores physically traumatic life memories for emotionally therapeutic purposes, such as promoting cathartic release, reframing attitudes, changing old habits and behavioral problems, and gaining conscious insight into the lessons of that life. Therapists use past life regression as one of the tools and techniques available to them to help clients resolve their problems. These therapists may call their practice Regression Therapy or Transformational Therapy.[9]

RELAXATION THERAPY: There are many methods and techniques to help you relax. Some help you relax your mind; others work primarily on the body. A few are designed as integrated systems for promoting body-mind-spirit harmony.

Some focus on complete muscular relaxation, some promote concentration, and others increase sensory awareness, all for the purpose of relaxation. It is up to you to find and choose the style that fits your needs and tastes.[10]

SELF-HYPNOSIS: Under the banner of self-hypnosis are a range of techniques similar to Zen meditation and Yoga. Dr. Roger Bernhardt, the co-author of *Self-Mastery through Self-Hypnosis* advocates the practice as follows:

I feel that self-hypnosis — has two distinct advantages over other mind-affecting exercises;

- A. Self-hypnosis is a time saver. Most other methods of altering consciousness call for periods of practice of twenty minutes or more. The self-hypnotic exercise requires approximately thirty seconds. That's not very much time when you consider the benefits such investment buys.

- B. Self-hypnosis is very specifically goal-oriented. You practice it with a definite purpose in mind; you want to change something within yourself. Although relaxation, serenity, decreased tension, and increased energy are common to all these other approaches, such results appear as beneficent side effects. However, in self-hypnosis, one may deliberately choose such a result via a post-hypnotic suggestion.[11]

References

1. *Alternative Medicine,* compiled by the Burton Goldberg Gp. (Payallut, WA.: Future Medicine Publishing Co., 1993), p. 63.
2. Ibid., p. 73.
3. Ibid., p. 244.
4. Ibid., p. 339.
5. Ibid., p. 346.
6. Ibid., p. 469.
7. Ibid., p. 306.
8. Kristin Guttschalk Olson, *Encyclopedia of Alternate Health Care* (New York, NY: Philip Lief Group, Inc., 1989), p. 76.
9. Ibid., p. 277.
10. Ibid., p. 255.
11. Roger Bernhardt & David Martin, *Self Mastery through Self-Hypnosis* (Indianopolis, IN.: Bobbs Merrill Co., 1977), p. 36.

CHAPTER 3
Your Mind in Hypnosis

"Let every man be fully persuaded in his own mind." ~Romans 14:5

For hundreds of years the world's greatest thinkers have strived to discover the intricacies involved in the numerous functions of the mind. We may concede that while man may never completely understand all of its mechanics, most knowledgeable professionals are in agreement that we *do* have a mind. Our minds are basically very powerful, and with proper programming, we can learn how to access the mind through positive affirmations, thereby improving our individual lifestyles. Remember, negative words act as barbs which tend to detract from both the trance and the positive suggestions being made.

Years before hypnosis as we recognize it today, and before Mesmer became known, Theophrastus Bombastus von Hohenheim Paracelsus (1493-1541) — described the powers of the mind. He described the trance state as follows:

> The Soul, in an ecstatic state, is self centered. The person is blind and deaf. His nose does not smell

anything, his hands feel nothing. Though he can see, he does not know what he sees. He may hear people talk but does not understand the words. He may grasp for something but is unconscious of what he holds in his hands. Such a person seems to be deprived of his senses and the world thinks he is an accomplished fool. In reality he is the wisest man before God, who lets him know His secrets better than all the wise men in the world.[1]

Many independent researchers have concluded that there are two levels of the mind, while other researchers have added additional dimensions. If we were to accept the two-level theory, then we can refer to both the *conscious mind* and the *subconscious (or the unconscious) mind*. Modern medical research links the functions of the conscious mind with that of the left brain, while the right hemisphere of the brain is responsible for our unconscious functions. With our conscious mind (the awareness mind), we think, analyze, rationalize, and perform numerous logical functions. That information which is then received by our visual, auditory, olfactory, and taste senses, is then immediately processed by the conscious mind. The conscious mind can accept, modify, or reject the input that may be utilized for immediate performance. However, when the inputs are deferred to future usage that acquired storage is maintained by the subconscious mind. Repetitious input, both positive and negative, will filter into the subconscious mind and have the tendency to become a permanent part of the individual's thought or thinking processes. The conscious mind functions as a vital element (that critical factor) with which we think, select, analyze, and constantly rationalize our tiniest situations and then render our subsequent actions.

The subconscious mind is the storehouse of memory. Information derived from one's thoughts is filed and stored in the subconscious mind, providing that your conscious mind accepts and acts upon the information it receives. Whether the nature of the data is good and positive or negative and detrimental, it is accepted—either deliberately or inadvertently. The data becomes an integral part of our inner self, thus affecting our emotions, our attitudes, our thinking, and ultimately our physical and mental health. Thus belief, imagination, and superstition may lead a person to become well and healthy, or conversely cause unnecessary sickness and illness.

The primary factor is how you program that computer segment of your mind. Paracelsus once wrote: "If a person believes in what I say, he will be sure that it will come true, and see it before his imagination. If he goes to bed with this idea strongly entrenched in his mind: he will experience exactly what I told him."[2]

Dr. Maxwell Maltz, author of *Psycho-Cybernetics*, was the first to advance the idea of cybernetics, which states that the subconscious works very much like a computer, acting through the brain. You are the programmer with the ability to program a positive product. As they say in the computer world, "GI=GO"—if you put *Garbage In*, you get *Garbage Out*. However one may alter that formula to read *Good in = Good Out*, so that our computerized mind will only function with positive results. Therefore instill positive thoughts within yourself and your computer will deliver positive, good actions. But if you program yourself negatively, negativity becomes an intrinsic part of your life.

The subconscious mind is the creative mind. It houses the archives and reference library of all information that might be recorded by our senses of sight, hearing, taste, touch, smell, and intuition. A person's subconscious mind is generally programmed by external sources. It does not differentiate between accurate or inaccurate data. For example, if the navigator of a large ocean liner were to program a course to a designated port with incorrect data, the ship would proceed to a wrong destination. But if the ship's navigator, upon discovering his error, could rectify his mistake by altering the programmed data, the ship would arrive at the desired destination. Therefore when we recognize, within our mental framework, that we have accepted erroneous data, we can make the changes that will result in a healthier, happier, and a more productive life.

Writing in *The Knack of Using Your Subconscious Mind*, author John K. Williams states:

> The subconscious mind works creatively upon whatever it is given by the conscious mind. Its nature is set and immutable. In the conscious aspect of personality we have spontaneous choice, volition, and originating action. In the subconscious, because of its nature, we have automatic reaction. The conscious mind is personal, while the subconscious mind is entirely impersonal.

Every person who has ever cultivated a garden should understand the two-fold aspect of mind, and the law under which it operates. The conscious mind plants the seed in the soil. It decides what kind of seed it will plant. The soil will, by the law of its being, germinate and nourish whatever is planted—roses or potatoes.

The subconscious mind is the soil, the medium, which by its nature, contains the elements necessary for birth and growth. By the law of its being, the subconscious mind will create and produce anything called for by the conscious mind. It is the nature of soil to bring forth, but it is not interested in what it brings forth. It does not know if the plant will bear strawberries or tomatoes. The whole economy and the universe would be disturbed and destroyed should the soil not act according to its nature.

The same is true of the subconscious mind. It is a *doer*, not a *knower*. It is intelligent without knowing, and is conscious only of its purpose and nature, but it is never self-conscious.[3]

The conscious mind can formulate judgments. The subconscious mind, which is almost void of the thought processes, only reacts, either in a positive and beneficial manner or in a negative and harmful manner. This reaction comes automatically without any degree of selective or calculated benefit values. Yet the subconscious mind is capable of overpowering the conscious. Rarely does either the conscious mind or the subconscious mind enter into the other's domain. When this does occur, disharmony prevails and a mental conflict arises. It results in confusion, poor decisions, headaches and even self-destruction through self-inflicted or natural causes.

In addition, it must be remembered that the conscious mind is the more energetic of the two worlds, while the subconscious mind is by far the more powerful. A knowledgeable person should take advantage of this fact and direct his efforts to the subconscious mind; because it is always the superior. *We may live without the conscious—but would perish without our subconscious mind.*

Bill Stiles in his book *Mind Power to Success* describes the power and the versatility of the subconscious mind:

1. **Sensation is controlled by the mind.** A hypnotized person can be told that he is either hot or cold and will react accordingly. If told he is hot, he will perspire and want to shed some clothing. If told he is cold, he will shiver and goose bumps will form on his skin. This is the subconscious mind believing and reacting to control the body.
2. **Pain can be induced or removed.** Many dentists are using hypnotism instead of chemical anesthetics. The mind believes what the dentist says and blocks the pain. In my own experiments I placed a piece of metal in a subject's hand and had the person concentrate on it while I told him that it was growing warmer and warmer. Then I suggested it was getting so hot that it was impossible to hold.

To the delight of the audience, the subject yelled "Ouch" and dropped the metal. This experiment was in all my shows, until one evening when a subject developed a blister on the palm of his hand. His body had reacted to the programming. The mind perceived the hot metal as real and sent a message to the hand which reacted physically and blistered. I learned a lesson. I never did that experiment again or say anything that could possibly cause a natural physical reaction.

3. **Habits can be broken.** Today, doctors are hypnotizing their patients to break old habits and establish substitutes, to reprogram away from the bad and toward the good. Many medical doctors use hypnotism to help patients lose weight or stop smoking.

4. **The subconscious can control activities.** Also in my shows, I would hypnotize audience members and have them sell imaginary newspapers or fish in an imaginary pond with an imaginary fishing rod. Even though the audience roared with laughter, these subjects seriously went about their tasks, their auto goal-finder clearly set in motion, their subconscious mind in control of their activities.

5. **The mind responds to posthypnotic suggestion.** While a person is hypnotized, his mind can be programmed to respond to a certain cue after he awakens. This is known as post hypnotic suggestion. The person wakes up, hears the cue, responds to it

but doesn't know why. He responds because his subconscious mind was programmed that way.

Basically, all of this means three things:
1. The hypnotic approach is very, very powerful.
2. You have been hypnotizing yourself into and out of things all your life.
3. You can monitor the hypnotic influences of your life and therefore control this wonderful power.[4]

Henry Bolduc describes the various factors of the mind as follows:

> The human mind has a creative factor and a critical factor, both of which are necessary for a healthy, productive life. The creative factor, the child of your subconscious mind, is as unquestioning as a computer, which complies with whatever information is programmed into it. Tell a computer that the world is flat, and it will "believe" this because it does not know any better. Yet this very naiveté can be a dynamic tool, because the creative factor of your mind truly believes you can do anything.
>
> The critical factor, a feature of your conscious mind, is more like the rudder of a ship. It can keep you on course and is the pilot of all your inhibitions. It sends such signals as "I can't." "I won't." Or "I haven't been able to before, so I can't now." Its influence is necessary when it reminds you, for example, of the folly of feeding crocodiles by hand. But it needs to be

overcome when it paralyzes you into crystallized habit patterns, when healthy caution becomes crippling fear. Ideally, your critical factor screens impulses, filters out what is harmful, and helps you set realistic goals.[5]

Alexander Cannon in *The Power Within* states:

Mind is ever the ruler of the Universe and of man within it; therefore it behooves each one of us to master oneself by controlling the mind-power within.

Through all recorded time the greatest of psychologists have preached this great truth to the entire world. From the days of Ovid to Disraeli that voice in the wilderness spoke over and over again, and in these days of war and anxiety one would do well to make Disraeli's suggestion his own. "Nurture your mind with great thoughts. To believe in the heroic makes heroes." Henley wrote, "I am the captain of my soul." And Webster said, "Mind is the great lever of all things." Ovid wisely stated, "It is the mind that makes the man." To know mind is to know God. Mind is greater than matter. The rejuvenation of the mind, including the inner mind is all-important, for the rejuvenation of the soul is the most important matter in the world; there is no conjurer like the human soul. Seek ye first the Kingdom of Mind (which is God) and all the things you want will be added unto you. This is an old Biblical truth that no change in religion, faith or future knowledge can alter, for that foundation is built upon the solid rock of fact and truth proved by experience.[6]

References

1. Harry M. Pachter, *Magic into Science* (New York, NY: Henry Schuman, 1951), p. 230.
2. Ibid., p. 232.
3. John K. Williams, *The Knack of Using Your Subconscious Mind* (Englewood Cliffs, NJ: Prentice Hall Inc., 1952), pp. 47-48.
4. Bill Stiles, *Mind Power to Success* (New Castle, PA:Stiles Associates, 1983), pp. 66-67.
5. Henry Leo Bolduc, "A Hypnotic Suggestion," *New Age Journal* (Jan-Feb. 1989).
6. Alexander Cannon, *The Power Within* (New York, NY: E. P. Dutton & Co., Inc., 1953), p. 201.

Other readings

Bailes, Frederick W. *Your Mind can Heal You.* New York, NY: Dodd, Mead & Co., 1941.

Masters, Roy. *How Your Mind Can Keep You Well.* Los Angeles, CA: Foundation of Human Understanding, 1971.

Delgado, Jose M. R. *Physical Control of the Mind.* New York, NY: Harper & Row Publishers, 1969.

CHAPTER 4
Mind-Body Connection

"Faith may work both ways, with the good it produces good works, but it leads the evil to evil works." ~Paracelsus

In the preceding chapter ("Your Mind in Hypnosis") we discussed the effects of your mind responding to self-hypnotic suggestions. Most people will readily agree that there is a corresponding relationship between our thoughts and our emotions or moods. We accept the premise that by maintaining a positive outlook and attitude we can expect more beneficial results in stress reduction and thereby obtain a more desirable lifestyle. We are aware that we can alter our emotions and moods by changing our outlook. However, there are still many skeptics who may accept our proven interaction with the mind and mental conditions, but who are very doubtful that the mind can have any effect on the physical body in promoting better health or in healing physical problems.

This negativism is not restricted to the lay person. Many professional medical personnel mock alternative medicine, self-hypnosis, etc. They refer to it as a lot of hogwash, superstition, and false hope. They know *absolutely* that the only way you can treat a disease is with the proper drugs. If the patient does not respond, they were going to die anyway. Perhaps, because of the fear of a malpractice lawsuit, they are only too willing to pronounce the death sentence on a patient. Some doctors may state that the patient has only had a few months to live, that the disease is terminal; or perhaps they bluntly tell a patient to go home and get their affairs in order. This is a detrimental use of negative suggestion.

Recently I counseled a woman in her early thirties who was attending a support group on "Dying with Dignity." The sessions were designed to prepare them for death. There was supposedly no hope of survival; and so accepting the inevitable, these unfortunates were preparing to die. The woman related to me that the group leader was disturbed with her attitude in expressing to the group that she did not wish to die with dignity but preferred to *live with dignity*. I congratulated her on the stand she was taking and advised her to avoid such negative contacts in the future. Her attitude and outlook soon improved dramatically.

Dr. Bernie Siegel relates examples of several specific case histories where physicians gave their patient an erroneous prognosis in the book, *Love, Medicine and Miracles*. Dr. Siegel discusses the healing partnership between the patient and the physician. He emphasizes that many physicians exercise poor judgment in offering a negative prognosis, informing the patient as to a projected time in which that patient can expect to live — or how soon he or she can anticipate death.

According to Dr. Siegel, this habitual practice of telling the patients, friends and loved ones how long a person has to live is a terrible mistake. Dr. Siegel remarks that ". . . it is a self-fulfilling prophecy. It must be resisted, even though many patients keep asking, 'How long?'"[1]

Most physicians are able to cite medical case histories where there are patients who overcome all statistics, recover, have complete remissions from "terminal" illnesses and continue to live a long normal lifespan. There are innumerable anecdotal instances where a terminally condemned patient, through positive thinking, belief in prayer and the practice of self-hypnosis has effected a cure after the medical community had abandoned hope.

Polly, a female client (age 42), was very talented in the application of self-hypnosis techniques, and had been undergoing the treatment of hepatitis for several years. Laboratory testing in February 1994 revealed that her tumor marker was at a critical high of 947 and unless it was lowered, she would be required to undergo a repeated course of extensive drug therapy. Polly's physician had follow-up tests scheduled for May. I suggested to her, in February, that she should apply self-hypnosis and visualize herself retiring to a very special room, her positive control room. In this imaginary room, she was to visualize a large indicator dial. This indicator would display the current "marker" numerical value, so that each time she applied self-hypnosis she would then check her current status and then deliberately lower the marker number a few appropriate points, towards her desired goal. Polly readily accepted the suggestions. In addition, she embellished the indicator by having the dial radiate different colors that would also indicate her progress. Red was the dangerous high and as the "marker" lowered, the colors changed, showing her progress, to a healthy violet-blue. Results of the May testing were not only extremely impressive to her physician, but also a wonderful relief to Polly, as the tumor marker level was reduced to 215. Self-hypnosis, using the C.R.I.B.S. method that will be covered in Chapter 6, can ensure positive results.

Our bodies have a natural immune system which is operational twenty-four hours a day to keep us healthy. Our natural immune system becomes activated when *virus-infected cells* and/or *tumor cells* develop within our bodies. They stimulate the *lymphocytes*, which in turn produce *interferons*. *Interferons* have the ability to inhibit the growth of *tumor cells*, to block viruses in the *virus-infected cells* and to transform some *lymphocytes* into *natural killer cells* whose prime purpose is to KILL the *tumor cells* and the *virus-infected cells*. The active *tumor cells* and *virus-infected cells* then reinitiate the entire immune cycle.

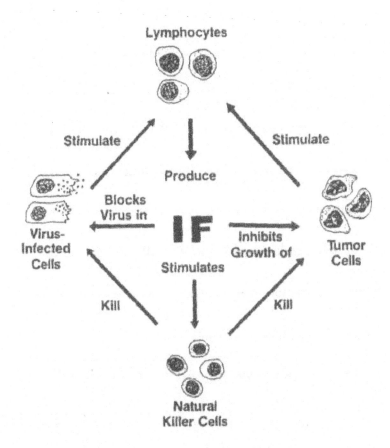

THE EFFECTS OF INTERFERON (IF)+

Viruses, virus-infected cells, and tumor cells stimulate lymphocytes to make interferon. Interferon then transforms other lymphocytes into natural killer cells, limits the growth of tumor cells, or blocks viral infection of other cells. Natural killer cells go on to destroy either virus-infected cells or tumor cells.

(Illustration from *Beating the Odds* by Marchetti)[2]

The idea that the subconscious mind can initiate the natural immune functions is not of recent origin. Hippollyte Bernheim (1837-1919) wrote about hypnotic suggestions converting ideo-sensory and ideo-motor reflexes into body functions. His book *Suggestive Therapeutics* was published in 1884 and later reprinted as *Hypnosis & Suggestion in Psychotherapy*. In it he states:

> The mechanism of suggestion in general, may then be summed up in the following formula: *increase of the reflex ideo-motor, ideo-sensitive, and ideo-sensorial excitability*. In the same way, through the effect of some influence, strychnine, for example, the sensitive-motor excitability is increased in the spinal cord, so that the least impression at the periphery of a nerve is immediately transformed into contracture, without the moderating influence of the brain being able to prevent this transformation. In the same way, in hypnotism, the ideo-reflex excitability is increased in the brain, so that any idea received is immediately transformed into an act, without the controlling portion of the brain, the higher centers, being able to prevent the transformation.[3]

The natural immune phenomenon does not occur without a control source. Our subconscious mind is the master control center. When the body is invaded by harmful bacteria or viruses, this information is transmitted to the subconscious mind by messenger cells. The subconscious mind directs the hypothalamus and the pituitary gland to activate the natural immune system. This is a very complex procedure encompassing many scientific studies. Readers desiring to pursue this subject in depth are referred to more definitive books such as:

- *Super Immunity: Master Your Emotions and Improve Your Health,* Pearsall
- *Mind-Body Therapy,* Rossi & Clark
- *The Psychobiology of Mind-Body Healing,* Rossi
- *Healing and the Mind,* Moyers
- *Beating the Odds,* Marchetti
- *Conscious Healing,* Selby
- *Head First,* Cousins

These books and others are listed at the end of this chapter.

Taking proper care of our bodies helps to further insure that we are keeping our immune system in proper order. Do not abuse your body by:

A. Subjecting your body to poisonous drugs, alcohol and tobacco.
B. Improper nutrition. One requires a healthy balanced diet. Fatty foods act as a poison to one's system.
C. Stress. Rest and relaxation are important in lowering stress.
D. Avoiding work or exercise.

A strong advocate for hypnosis, Dr. Albert Marchetti, author of *Beating the Odds,* states:

> Hypnosis can also be used as an escape that breaks the cycle of fear, cancer, and more fear, or of

depression, cancer, and more depression. It can allow the mind to relax, to let go of the problem and temporarily shift the focus to something or someone else. This escape or temporary release will set up the conditions for a remission. It will allow the mind to shift from the BAD SYSTEM to the GOOD SYSTEM and in so doing generate the chemicals that destroy cancer cells.

Hypnosis can work in other ways as well. For example, in combination with other therapies or as the driving force behind those therapies. Take, for instance, the case (in chapter 11) of the young boy who fought his brain tumor with self-directed visualization. He performed the mental imagery in a couple of sessions each day. He was also instructed in a form of hypnotic suggestion, to continue to fight the tumor mentally and physically, hour after hour, day after day, asleep or awake. As you will recall, his success could have been attributed to a number of different things, but most likely, it was the combination of them all, including the verbal suggestion.

In combination with the standard treatments of surgery, radiation, and chemotherapy, hypnotic suggestion can increase the potency of these treatments while, at the same time, bolstering the power of the natural defense system. Hypnosis is the most potent form of the healing word, and can be used to fill the void of purely psychologically directed cures. Since the practice has already been shown to work within the constraints of its limited use, imagine the potential in years to come when current techniques are improved. Hypnosis is definitely the cancer cure of mind over matter. It is yesterday's and tomorrow's cure that can be used today.[4]

Charles Tebbitts in *Miracles on Demand* extols the virtues of hypnosis when he writes:

> Health Maintenance is inherent in hypnotism because the body normalizes itself to a great extent when hypnotized. Also, the power of disruptive emotions can be minimized, thereby reducing stress. The stress caused by destructive emotions such as anger, hatred, resentment or fear often impairs the natural functioning of the immune system and is, therefore, often the indirect cause of physical illness.
>
> At the age of eighty years I enjoy good health. I have not had a cold or the flu for over ten years even though I constantly come in contact with people who suffer with them. I regard myself as living proof that the immune system, if not interfered with, is a near-perfect defense system. I am not a guru and I do not wear a turban or a purple robe. I am a normal human being who has learned to control the involuntary functions of my body with hypnosis, thereby allowing my immune system to operate as nature intended. I own my own adrenal gland, and I make all decisions as to how angry I get and how I will deal with it. I certainly will not allow it to disrupt my glandular system and break down my immune system.[5]

Positive suggestions, visualization, and every belief have a profound effect on the subconscious mind. A hypnotized person touched by a cube of ice, or even a fingertip, and told that he/she was being burned with a red hot iron, could produce a painful blister. A healthy man, in a hypnotic state, when given a negative suggestion that his leg was paralyzed, could find when awakened that he could no longer move that leg. When your subconscious mind accepts a suggestion, that suggestion becomes reality.

References

1. Bernie Siegel, *Love, Medicine & Miracle* (New York, NY: Harper and Row, 1986), p. 38.
2. Albert Marchetti, *Beating the Odds* (Chicago, IL: Contemporary Books, 1988), p. 51.
3. H. Bernheim, MD, *Hypnosis – Suggestion in Psychotherapy* (New Hyde Park, NY: University Books, 1964), pp. 138-139.
4. Marchetti, pp. 184-185.
5. Charles Tebbetts, *Miracles on Demand* (Glendale, CA: Westwood Publishing Co., 1987, pp. 108-109.

Other readings

Cousins, Norman. *Head First.* New York, NY: E. P. Dutton, 1989.

Moyers, Bill. *Healing and the Mind.* New York, NY: Doubleday, 1993.

Pearsall, Paul *Super Immunity.* New York, NY: Fawcett Gold Medal, 1988

Selby, John. *Conscious Healing.* New York, NY. Bantam Books, 1989.

Rossi, Ernest L. & Cheek, David B. *Mind-Body Therapy.* New York, NY: W. W. Norton & Co.,1988.

Dossey, Larry. *Healing Words.* San Francisco CA, Harper, 1993.

Rossi, Ernest L. *The Psychobiology of Mind-Body Healing.* New York,NY: W. W. Norton & Co., 1986.

Chopra, Deepak. *Ageless Body, Timeless Mind.* New York, NY: Harmony Books, 1993.

_____. *Quantum Healing.* New York, NY: Bantam Books, 1990.

CHAPTER 5
Mastery of Self- Hypnosis

"Great works are performed not by strength, but by perseverance."
~Samuel Johnson

Emile Coué is considered by many to be the father of self-hypnosis. He repeatedly denied that his method, which he called auto-suggestion, had anything to do with hypnotism. He believed that it differed from hypnotism because he did not stare into a patient's eyes and thereby transfer his personality into the patient—an erroneous belief generally associated with hypnosis at that time.

Emile Coué was born February 26, 1857, in Troyes, a city in east-central France, about one hundred miles southwest of Nancy. His railroad worker father was able to send him to study at the Paris School of Pharmacy, and to provide a modest capital with which he opened his own drug store in Troyes in 1882. Becoming interested in what he was hearing about Liébeault's and Bernheim's successes in drug-free treatment of patients, and having himself seen the curative effect of a placebo he gave to a customer who kept demanding a drug he was not authorized to sell, Coué went to Nancy during the winter of 1885-86 and stayed for several weeks, closely observing what was being done.

In 1896, he retired as a practicing pharmacist and devoted the remainder of his life to the understanding and advancement of hypnotism. After several years of deliberation and continued practice, he decided that Dr. Liébeault's procedure was unsatisfactory because of its lack of method. His continuing study of this relatively new science included, among other sources of available information, an American correspondence course. Shortly thereafter, his attitude seems to have changed in his concept of hypnosis. Until then he had believed that the hypnotist implanted suggestions into the mind of the patient while the individual was *unconscious*. Now, however, Coué required that his subjects offer specific suggestions to themselves while they were entirely *conscious*.

Coué taught that his method was simplicity itself. So basic was his procedure that it was scoffed at, as are all simple solutions of seemingly complicated problems. But its logic is irrefutable, and its effects are demonstrated every day of our lives.

Coué's auto-suggestion formula:

> All that is necessary is to place oneself in a condition of mental passiveness, silence the voice of conscious analysis, and then deposit into the ever-awake subconscious that idea or suggestion which one desires to be realized. Every night, after you have been comfortably settled in bed and are on the point of dropping off to sleep, murmur in a low but clear voice, just loud

enough to be heard by yourself, this little formula: "Every day, in every way, I am getting better and better." Recite this phrase like a litany, twenty times or more. In order to avoid distracting your attention by the effort of counting, it would be an excellent idea to tick the number off on a piece of string tied in twenty knots.[1]

Many leading proponents of hypnotism acted against Monsieur Coué, for various reasons. Perhaps it was because Coué was removing some of the mysticism from the hypnotic process, or conceivably because they presumed that if individuals could do it themselves it would eliminate the necessity of employing the professional services of a hypnotist or hypnotherapist.

During my many years of practice I was unjustly criticized for teaching self-hypnosis. A peer group that I was associated with thought it was dangerous for people to learn too much about the subject of hypnotism; but primarily they opposed it because it might then detract from their professional income.

Coué's suggested method was to have the patients repeat over and over the simple phrase mentioned above, as a formula to self-help. In the original French, "*Tous les jours, à tous points de vue, je vais de mieux en mieux.*" The English version which Coué considers most satisfactory is, "Every day, in every way, I am getting better and better."[2] He recommended that the individual recite this verbalism twenty or more times each day. I have applied this procedure in many cases with a slight but effective variation, by accentuating each progressive word, each time the phrase was recited:

- *Every* day, in every way, I am getting better and better.
- Every *day*, in every way, I am getting better and better.
- Every day, *in* every way, I am getting better and better.
- Every day, in *every* way, I am getting better and better.
- Etc.

This simple variation tends to concentrate the client's attention and readily conveys more meaning and greater impact. It also eliminates the necessity of counting, as they only need to repeat the process twice.

Certain other hypnotists have changed the wording to be: "Every day, in every way, *with GOD'S help*, I am getting better and better."

Many years ago I was visited by a client who was suffering from phantom pains emanating from his knee, from a leg that had been amputated at the hip. This man, in his mid-40s, was a professor at a local university. The amputation was performed approximately one year prior to the time he requested my services. The severity and persistency of the pain had prevented him from returning to his profession. His physician referred him to a prominent and respected hypnotist who failed to alleviate the man's pain and suffering. He advised the distraught professor to recite those words, "Every day, in every way, I am getting better and better." This repetition of words merely aggravated his condition. Several weeks later the professor arranged an appointment with me. During our first interview, I asked if he had ever experienced hypnosis. He stated, in a very disgusted tone of voice, what the other hypnotist had advised him to do. He continued, "I feel as if I were being treated as an illiterate child."

Understanding the distressed client's situation and quandary, I explained the Coué Method and assured him that there was no intent, on the part of the earlier hypnotist, to question his intellect. I further explained that in the past 50 years, innumerable people had benefited by this type of suggestion. In the course of the forthcoming trance, the professor proved himself to be a good subject, and following that with a few moments of suggestions the pain ceased and the tight drawn look upon his face disappeared. When the session was finished, he appeared as a completely new person. His concerned wife remarked that this was the first time she had seen him smiling since the operation.

I believe that by saying the phrase, "Every day, in every way, I am getting better and better," has merit. Some situations change instantly, while others need time to take root. If the subject sincerely believes that they are becoming better and better each and every day — *they will.*

Hyman A. Lewis of the Lewis Hypnosis Training Center developed a different self-hypnosis system based upon the letters of the alphabet. A - B - C - D - E - F - G and H are all to be used as a frame of reference for entering the stages of hypnosis. A to C indicate the beginning of effective relaxation of the body and the mind; the letters D to F, the medium stage of subconscious receptivity; and the completion of F to H, the stage in which to readily incorporate effective positive suggestions.

The procedure:

Make yourself comfortable. Be sure your clothing is loose as you are seated in a comfortable chair in the privacy of your room. Close your eyes after breathing deeply a few times to establish an easy rhythm or relaxation "set" and state the following to yourself. . . . In a moment I will use the letters of the alphabet as a guide to elicit the state of uncritical acceptance to suggestion. A . . . I place my attention upon the muscles around my eyes which are beginning to relax . . . this easy flow of relaxation affects every muscle and nerve and fiber of my muscles to a degree of utter relaxation. . . I allow this feeling to spread to my closed eyelids which are becoming heavy . . . so . . . so very heavy . . . drowsy . . . becoming drowsier and drowsier, sleepy, as if my eyes want to sleep. . . . I now feel as if it would take a superhuman effort on my part to open my eyes. . . . I try to open them but I cannot. B . . . I allow the feelings of relaxation to flow through my body from the top of my head down to the tips of my toes. It is such a wonderful feeling of comfort and calm as to allow the feelings of relaxation to flow upwards from my toes to the arch and heel of my feet. This steady stream of relaxation courses through my ankles and into the calves of my legs. My legs feel heavy, comfortable, and relaxed. The feelings of relaxation begin to deepen as it moves upward and through the large muscles of my thighs, into the region of my hips and now so gently to my diaphragm. I begin to concentrate on my breathing and find that it has become gentle and smooth. The very rhythm of my breathing produces deeper feelings of calm as the relaxation continues to course through the region of my chest. Every fiber of my muscles there, relax. This calm . . . comfortable feeling, moves into the area of my shoulder muscles there, relax. Every muscle is becoming flaccid and inert. This comfortable feeling moves through my arms and down to my fingertips while every breath is making me feel more sleepy . . . more relaxed. C . . . This comfortable feeling of relaxation now touches every muscle, nerve and fiber of the muscles of my neck and my head now moves easily forward onto my chest. I am going deeper and deeper. D . . . into a deep hypnotic sleep, where I shall always remain fully aware but concentrated and focusing only on specific suggestions. When I state the letter E . . . it will be the signal to feel equally relaxed in body and mind. F . . . I am now in this wonderful state but desire to go even deeper. The letters G and H . . . will mean that I am in a self-hypnosis state as the letter H will stand for hypnosis. G . . . H. I am now in a state of subconscious receptivity and give myself the following suggestions. . . . Each time I utilize this technique for hypnosis I will go deeper and deeper (which is in effect a post-hypnotic suggestion). It is wise to remain in this state a few moments to experience and enjoy the profound relaxation. As this is an exercise to produce deeper states of self-hypnosis it would not be wise at this time to suggest anything more than your desire to elicit more effective subsequent states.[3]

The method by Hyman Lewis is very effective. To make it easier to remember — as easy as remembering the A-B-Cs — I have modified the suggested method to teach my students, as follows:

A - *Attention,* all of my *attention* and my *awareness* is being directed to my muscles, ligaments and tendons. . . . I *allow* my mind and body to relax and release tension. . . . I *allow* my eyes to get heavier and drowsier . . . so tired they want to close.

B – *Believing* that I can control my *behavior*, my emotions and my actions, I visualize my mind achieving a more relaxed state as my *body* continues to relax, allowing the relaxation to flow throughout my arms and legs. From the tip of my toes, and fingers, and to my shoulders, I am releasing all tension. . . . I am *becoming better and better* every day.

C – *Comfortable*, and I am in *control*, as my body *continues* to relax. This *calmness* and *comfort continues* to permeate every fiber of my body to release its tensions. My *concentration* is focused on total and *complete* relaxation. I am a *confident* person.

D – *Deeper* and *deeper* into a profound state of hypnotic relaxation. *Dropping* into *depths* of physical release and allowing mental stress or worry to *disappear*.

E – *Every* cell is responding, my *entire* body is relaxing. *Each* positive suggestion becomes more pronounced and accepted. *Effortlessly*, I permit my mind to release its binding tensions and its negative *energies*. I am entirely *energized* with profound *enthusiasm*.

F – *Flowing* quietly, smoothly, I am *focusing* my thoughts on *favorable* and desired objectives. My body *feels* like it is *floating* along on a *fantastic* voyage. I am *feeling fine*.

G – *Goals* are *getting* established in my subconscious mind. I am *glad* that I have the desire and capability to achieve this *golden* state of hypnosis. I really feel *good* and have a *great* attitude. I am *getting* ready, on the next letter of H to enter that *great* state of hypnosis.

H – *HYPNOSIS*, a wonderful state of awareness, *higher* response and stronger direction towards my positive *healthy* goals. Each and every time I enter the state of SELF-HYPNOSIS now and in the future, I will become more and more proficient and reach higher levels of concentration with total relaxation. **Hypnosis is happiness.**

It is unnecessary to remember the exact wording as you start reciting the alphabet; only follow the cue words and allow them to act as your guide in more readily achieving the desired relaxation of the hypnotic state.

Dr. Paul Adams, a noted authority on self-hypnosis, says:

The biggest barrier in achieving self-hypnosis is not knowing how to recognize the state of hypnosis. Therefore, I am going to repeat some very important facts for your guidance.
1. Hypnosis is a normal, natural state.
2. You do not fall asleep or become unconscious.
3. Hypnosis is a narrowing of the attention span to primarily one thing.
4. It is an altered state of consciousness.
5. It is a state of hyper-suggestibility.
6. The only real proof of genuine, effective hypnosis of self-hypnosis is the post-hypnotic response.[4]

References

1. Emile Coué, *My Method* (Garden City, NY: Doubleday, Page & Co., 1923), p. 26.
2. Harry C. Brooks, *The Practice of Autosuggestion* (New York, NY: Dodd, Mead & Co., 1922), p. 79.
3. Hyman A. Lewis, *Self-Hypnosis Dynamics* (Oak Park, MI: Lewis Hypnosis & Training Center, 1962), pp. 40-42.
4. Adams, *The New SELF-HYPNOSIS* (N. Hollywood, CA: Wilshire Book Co., 1967), p. 36.

Other readings

Hunter, Roy C. *The Art of Hypnosis*. Merrimack, NH: National Guild of Hypnotists, 1994.

Soskis, David A. *Teaching Self-Hypnosis*. New York, NY: W. W. Norton & Co., 1986.

CHAPTER 6
My Formula for Successful Self-Hypnosis

"Fix your thought closely on what is being said, and let your mind enter fully into what is being done, and into what is doing it."
~ Marcus Aurelius

I have developed a formula called C.R.I.B.S. that has proven to be highly effective in teaching self-hypnosis to thousands of my students and clients. **C.R.I.B.S.** is an acronym for *Commitment, Relaxation, Imagery, Belief and Suggestion*. These are the essential keys that, when properly applied, will result in achieving the mastery of self-hypnosis.

Each key is to be considered of equal importance, as the benefits of self-hypnosis will not manifest themselves with the shortening or omission of any one of them. You may ponder the words and, in your estimation, one factor may supersede another in effective value or importance. As an illustration, imagine in your mind's eye a wagon wheel with five spokes (each spoke representing a requirement of self-hypnosis). Decide which of the spokes is the most important, and what could happen to the wheel if just one spoke was shortened or eliminated?

The reader is strongly advised to read Chapter 7 – Commitment, Chapter 8 – Relaxation, Chapter 9 – Imagery, Chapter 10 – Belief and Chapter 11 – Suggestions. If you plan to use a CD recorder follow the instructions in Chapter 11.

When you are prepared and have attained that state of expectancy, you are ready to start your venture into that almost magical world of self-hypnosis.

I have titled this technique or procedure, "THE FORTY COUNT METHOD OF ATTAINING SELF-HYPNOSIS."

1. Retire to a quiet, darkened room where you will not be disturbed.
2. Loosen any tight or restrictive clothing and remove your shoes.
3. Lie on a bed, sofa or reclining chair.
4. Tighten the muscles in your legs, apply as much tension as you can, hold the tension and count backwards from 10 to 2, take a deep breath, and at the count of 1, exhale slowly. Permit the muscles in your legs to slowly relax—relax completely. Feel and become aware of the last bit of residual tension fading away.
5. Extend your arms upward, tighten the muscles of your forearms and upper arms, and clench your fists. Repeat the same counting procedure that you did for your legs.
6. Tighten the muscles within your abdomen and chest, bearing down as hard as you can. Repeat the same counting procedure as you did for your legs and arms.
7. Lastly, close your eyes tightly, tighten your jaw muscles, clench your teeth together, swallow, and

then apply tension to your neck and throat muscles. Repeat the same counting procedure. *At this point you should have accomplished complete physical relaxation; however, should you continue to still feel physical tension, repeat steps 4, 5, 6, & 7. With a little practice you will become very proficient in developing complete control over tensions and stresses of your physical body.*

8. After having mastered the state of complete physical relaxation, you are again ready to proceed by relaxing your mental self. Start counting, backwards, from 40. Many individuals prefer counting an inhale as 40, the exhale as 39, inhale 38, exhale 37, etc. You may even visualize erasing the numbers from a blackboard as you say them. With each count, permit yourself to mentally relax by imaging a perfect vacation, a golf game or whatever imparts to you a satisfying and relaxed feeling. Continue this count down until you have reached the number 25. At 25 we pause on our magical plateau. Stop counting and implant into your mind the mental images, your unfulfilled goals, and that which you desire to accomplish. How long you remain at this plateau is optional. For some, perhaps as little time as five minutes will suffice, while others may remain and luxuriate for 20 or 30 minutes.

9. To exit this state of mind, you may prefer to doze off into a peaceful, restful, and rejuvenating sleep, awakening at a specified time feeling rested, invigorated, or revitalized. You will be ready to enjoy a more posi-

tive and self-directed life. However, if practicing this procedure at other than your regular sleeping time, you may easily bring yourself out of your self-imposed trance by continuing to reverse the count from 24 towards 1. As you count back, perceive the feeling of relaxation with a fresh alertness, revitalized body, and a greater positive outlook. When you reach the number 5, breathe a little deeper while your body continues to absorb that fresh positive energy. Then feel more and more stimulated. At the count of 1, EYES WIDE OPEN — A WONDERFUL FEELING — ENJOY LIFE TO ITS UTMOST.

10. CAUTION – Once you commence counting backwards from 40, avoid allowing anything or anyone to distract you. Do not open your eyes, nor attempt to arise and move. Program your subconscious mind to accept the reality of turning over compete control to your inner self. You cannot react consciously to any given situation until you reach that 5-4-3-2- and – 1 – eyes open! Plan for the event of an emergency situation. If someone should start knocking on your door, or the telephone should ring, you must terminate the session. Quickly but methodically resume the countdown back to one. For example, if you were on the count of 32 when the interruption occurred, mentally say "30-25-20-15-10" and then "5-4-3-2-1 – eyes open." To properly condition the subconscious mind, it is imperative that once you start the countdown from 40 you must always count back to 5-4-3-2 and 1. The count back is not necessary

when you are leaving the magic plateau at 25 to enter your evening's sleep. The countdown from 24 to 1 is an energizing experience and is designed to vitalize and energize. Use it for wakening up; do not count back when you are entering a state of slumber.

Another advantage in practicing the "Forty Count Method" is that you can shorten the time usually required to reach the self-hypnosis state. While most recommended methods approximate these same time frames, reciting the same words or performing the same tasks each time you wish to employ self-hypnosis, the "Forty Count Method" can be shortened as your proficiency increases.

While you progress, you will realize that you may not need to count back from 10 to 1 each time, with the arms, legs, trunk and head, to attain a complete state of physical relaxation. This process can be reduced by tensing the arms and legs simultaneously, then counting back from 10 to 1. The same process is repeated for the trunk and head together. Now we have shortened the time of the physical relaxation by 50%. You can further shorten the required time by tensing the arms, legs, trunk and head all together and then counting from 10 to 1. Now the time has been reduced by 75%. If you fully apply yourself and are becoming fully relaxed, the process can be further decreased by tensing all four parts and counting back from 5 to 1. Some of the more skilled students have reached the ultimate state by taking a deep breath on the count of two, tightening all four parts, and exhaling on the count of one. Complete physical relaxation should be achieved in only a matter of seconds.

The mental relaxation portion, starting after physical relaxation, can be abbreviated by starting your count back at 35 instead of 40. If your results are favorable, you may commence by counting from 30. Again the more skilled adepts may take a breath at 26, exhale at 25, and thereby enter that wonderful MAGICAL PLATEAU. Avoid rushing this process. If you are not reaching the ultimate in a completely relaxed mental and physical state, just return to the original process described earlier.

CHAPTER 7
Commitment

Persistence:
"Nothing in the world can take the place of persistence: Talent will not; nothing is more common than unsuccessful men with talent. Genius will not; unrewarded genius is almost a proverb. Education will not; the world is full of educated derelicts. Persistence and determination alone are omnipotent."

~ Calvin Coolidge

Learning can be a simple uncomplicated undertaking or it can become an extremely complicated and frustrating struggle. The individual who is about to learn must first be motivated. It could be the "what's in it for me" attitude, the hope of monetary gain, or possibly a quest to satisfy curiosity. Whatever the motive is, it is important. For without a goal, one does not have the initiative to learn. Why did you pick up this book? What are your expectations? What do you expect to gain financially? Are you sincerely interested in applying the principles of self-hypnosis to improve yourself? Is it your personal quest to satisfy a bit of curiosity that may have been lingering in the recesses of your mind for years? Once your motives become established, are you prepared to make a sound commitment?

The study of self-hypnosis is not a touch-and-go whim, but rather a process requiring your commitment and dedication to adhere to, and practice, the principles outlined in this program.

We are a nation of individuals who expect to learn about things *now*. We want to read a textbook and have all the answers *now*. This attitude of expecting immediate results does not work when dealing with the subconscious mind. Your subconscious mind is the perfect servant (or master) of your actions, emotions and attitudes. The Law of Reverse Effect is dominant, and the more one tries to force data into or withdraw information from the subconscious, the more your mind will balk and rebel. Your endeavors will thus become more difficult or impossible. We have all felt the frustration of trying to recall a specific topic, usually to remark that the answer was on the tip of our tongue, but we could not grasp that particular thought. The greater our effort, the more vexed our minds became, even to the extent of becoming blank. Later, after we have succumbed to the pressure of trying, the answer unexpectedly appears in our consciousness.

Bill T. (male 71 years old) was a retired minister, now teaching part-time at a Southern university. Suffering from a cancerous tumor in his chest, his condition had deteriorated to the point that he could not walk; he was in extreme pain and resigned to his impending demise.

I had known this man for years and invited him to Pittsburgh for a weekend of self-hypnosis. After meeting him at the airport I had to transport Bill in a wheelchair to my car.

During that weekend I hypnotized Bill several times and taught him the basic essentials of visualization and suggestions for self-hypnosis. Knowing that he served proudly in the Marines during World War II, participating in several beachhead landings and battles during the campaign of the Pacific, I directed my suggestions and scenario for visualization toward that impressive period. Bill was the epitome of that "once a Marine always a Marine" cliché. His experiences during those Marine years impacted the next fifty years of his life.

The script that I prepared for him described a paradise of an island where the natives lived peacefully in a proverbial Garden of Eden. This utopia was invaded by a hostile force and Marine Sgt. Bill was charged with the mission of invading the island and destroying the enemy forces. As I talked to Bill, describing his initiative, his determination, his commitment and his relentlessness in seeking out and destroying the hostile forces, I observed his unconscious reactions. His facial expression reflected each phase of the challenge: the determination and seriousness of the landing, the ensuing battle and the final victory smile. This story was purely allegorical, and I didn't have to mention his body, the invasion of the cancer cells or his ability to fight and conquer.

Following the sessions he demonstrated a marked improvement, refused to take pain pills, moved more freely and became more relaxed.

Bill was instructed in several self-hypnosis procedures and was given a tape of our sessions.

Returning to the airport several days later, Bill walked upright and insisted upon carrying his own luggage. His recovery progressed rapidly, and within two weeks he resumed teaching at the university and returned as a substitute preacher.

Investment ensures commitment. If, for example, an individual were to attend a course in self-hypnosis that was quite expensive, then that person would apply themselves much more readily in their studies to ensure they received their money's worth. If the same subject were presented at a Community College at a very reasonable charge, to the money-motivated individual this would be a small investment. The attitude then becomes, "What if I do miss a session or two? It only costs a couple of bucks for the evening ."

A hypothetical situation was presented to many of my classes in self-hypnosis. "How many of you would be interested in a program that would cost you absolutely nothing, but would guarantee that you would lose weight, stop smoking, reduce stress or whatever else you desired?" Each time, almost every hand would be raised. Then I would explain that during the following week, each person wishing to take advantage of this offer should bring in a legal-sized envelope. On the outside they were to print their names, and their desired objectives or goals. Inside would be placed thirty 100-dollar bills ($3000.) This was their money. I was only going to hold it for them. I would offer my total support to ensure their success in reaching their goals. At the end of a given time period and finding the goals successfully attained, the envelope and money would be faithfully returned. If they were to fail, the money would be forfeited.

Since this was only a hypothetical situation, no one submitted an envelope or accepted the offer. Can you imagine a person lighting up a cigarette, knowing that it would cause them to forfeit $3000? People will forfeit their health, success, happiness, and even their very lives but are very hesitant when the issue involves money.

Think of a person whose goal is to lose thirty pounds within a six-month period. Perhaps during the first three months, not a single pound is lost; but as the deadline nears, the thirty pounds would, indeed, be sweated away. Yes, the motivation of monetary loss or gain can be a very effective factor in both one's conscious and subconscious mind.

CHAPTER 8
Relaxation

"A happy life begins with tranquility of mind." ~ Cicero

Learning the art of relaxation may be one of the most important accomplishments that can bring about major improvements in the quality of our lives.

In America, hundreds of millions of dollars are wasted purchasing relaxation drugs. We disburse more capital on these questionable drugs in our illustrious nation (the most desirable and livable country in the world) than in all other countries combined. Is it true that our lives are made stressful through circumstance; or rather do we subconsciously believe this to be so? In addition to the money spent on valium and other drugs, ponder the millions of dollars that are spent on therapists, psychiatrists, psychologists, counselors, etc. Pursuing that ever-elusive magical relaxation subtracts millions of man-hours from our national productive time. Though the goal is elusive, we do have the ability within ourselves to direct our actions. Self-hypnosis is another tool of our mind and we must learn to harness its potential.

Relaxation is one of the easiest and also one of the most beneficial applications of self-hypnosis. When you understand that you, alone, are causing the stress and tension within yourself, you will realize that if **you can bring it on, you can also release it.**

The problem is that stress can bring about heart problems, ulcers, headaches, stomach disorders, constipation, colitis and many other maladies. Learn to relax by refusing to accept those situations that have caused and promoted your tensions. If you refuse to accept it, then it is not there to bother you. Anyone can achieve relaxation providing they are willing to release the stress and tension within themselves.

Why would we want to put ourselves into a stressful situation? Dr. Herbert Benson, in discussing the fight-or-flight response, states:

> Humans, like other animals, react in a predictable way to acute and chronic stressful situations, which trigger an inborn response that has been part of our physiologic makeup for perhaps millions of years. This has been popularly labeled the "fight-or-flight" response. When we are faced with situations that require adjustments of our behavior, an involuntary response increases our blood pressure, heart rate, rate of breathing, blood flow to the muscles and metabolism, preparing us for conflict or escape.
>
> This innate fight-or-flight reaction is well recognized in animals. A frightened cat standing with arched back and hair on end, ready to run or fight; an enraged dog with dilated pupils, snarling at his adversary; an

African gazelle running from a predator; all are responding by activation of the fight-or-flight response. Because we tend to think of man in Cartesian terms, as essentially a rational being, we have lost sight of his origins and of his Darwinian struggle for survival where the successful use of the fight-or flight response was a matter of life or death.

Man's ancestors with the most highly developed fight-or-flight reactions had an increased chance of surviving long enough to reproduce. Natural selection favored the continuation of the response. As progeny of ancestors who developed the response over millions of years, modern man almost certainly still possesses it.

In fact, the fight-or-flight response, with its bodily changes of increased blood pressure, rate of breathing, muscle blood flow, metabolism, and heart rate, has been measured in man. Situations that demand that we adjust our behavior elicit this response. It is observed, for example, among athletes prior to a competitive event. But the response is not used as it was intended—that is, in preparation for running or fighting with an enemy. Today, it is often brought on by situations that require behavioral adjustments, and *when not used appropriately, which is most of the time, the fight-or-flight response repeatedly elicited may ultimately lead to the dire diseases of heart attack and stroke.*[1]

You have the choice of fighting or running, you also have the option of accepting or rejecting a stressful situation.

A scenario I wish to describe is that of clients imagining themselves attending a picnic. A person baking potatoes in a grill is bent over the burning embers, raking the newly baked steaming *hot potatoes* out of the ashes. As you approach, this individual, who is wearing asbestos gloves, picks up a *hot potato*, calls your name and quickly tosses the *hot potato* directly to you. Question: do you catch it, and sear or blister your hands? If so, who is responsible for the burn—the one who tossed it to you? Or is it you for being so foolish as to catch it?

Whenever a *hot potato* is tossed to you, you have three choices. First, catch it and get burned; second, step aside and let the potato drop harmlessly to the ground, and after it cools, you may pick it up; or, your third choice, bat it directly back to the person who tossed it to you.

Hot potatoes are those little situations or circumstances in life that cause the many tensions found within most of us. Learn to play the hot potato game properly and you can eliminate a major negative factor. Eliminating stress, can improve your health and your quality of life.

Being what is commonly referred to as "uptight" does not impress anyone. Bragging about how many hours one spends on professional help is hardly impressive either. Almost all of my clients who have complained of stress or stress-related problems have been involved in an extremely stressful occupation. I have heard this complaint from countless people employed in almost every profession and career imaginable. During a major winter snowstorm I was visited by a client who was a captain of a large passenger jet. During the course of the pre-hypnosis session I questioned him as to whether flying under adverse weather conditions had affected him, causing him stress. He laughed amiably and replied that flying was the most relaxing activity he ever performed and that the only time he felt tension was when he was driving along the Pittsburgh Parkway leading to the airport. **Stress is found where we wish to place it and is cultured by our own mind.**

When people state that they cannot relax, is it a matter of whether they can't, or whether **they elect to retain their state of tension?**

References

1. Herbert Benson, MD, *The Relaxation Response* (New York, NY: Avon, 1976), pp. 23-25.

Other readings

Roon, Karin. *Karin Roon's New Way to Relax.* New York, NY: Greystone Press, 1961.

Jacobson, Edmund. *You Must Relax.* New York, NY: McGraw-Hill Book Co., 1957.

Edmonston, William E. Jr. *Hypnosis and Relaxation.* New York, NY: John Wiley & Sons, 1981.

CHAPTER 9
Imagery and Imagination

"Image may or may not represent external reality, but it always represents internal reality." ~ Martin L. Rossman, MD

To image or imagine is the ability to mentally visualize your ideas, accomplishments, goals, and objectives. When the novice is first introduced to self-hypnosis they occasionally remark, in honest perplexity, "I cannot see or feel anything." Imagery may be conceptualized in many different impressions. While some individuals may visualize in color, others will do so only in black and white. Some images may not be visual but instead be perceived more as a thought or memory.

Bolduc, in discussing visualization, writes:

> Creative visualization, also called guided imagery, is another tool for programming the inner mind. It adds a new dimension to a hypnotic suggestion. By using the mind's eye to picture positive actions and

positive results, you can point your mind in the direction you want your life to go.

Visualization covers a broad spectrum, ranging from fantasy images to vivid, colorful mental movies. Visual impressions can come in colored pictures, in black-and-white pictures, and in pictures not quite tangible. For some, these impressions may be like a movie with the person as the star of the show. The person also directs the scenes, actions, and dialogues. For others, impressions may come as feelings or vibrations.

Seeing your goal as already accomplished is perhaps the most dynamic tool of mental imagery. This is a big step toward your goal's actual fulfillment because it bridges the gap between your inner-world reality and your outer-world reality. Using the example of public speaking, there is one way to apply this principle: "I now picture myself after the talk. People are coming up and thanking me, saying how much they enjoyed and learned from the talk. As they are shaking my hand, I realize that I truly did well. I did do a good job and am thankful for the experience of helping others and speaking with them."[1]

Do you dream, or daydream, in color, or are your dreams restricted only to black and white? Many people flatly state that they cannot visualize. When questioned they can very easily describe their home or loved ones in graphic detail. When they describe a beautiful vacation spot they are drawing from memory recall, which is visualization.

IMAGERY AND IMAGINATION

Imagery can be enhanced by not only recalling the visual aspects of the subject but by using the other senses:
- What did it look like?
- What did it smell like?
- What did it taste like?
- What did it feel like?
- What did it sound like?

If you were to imagine a vacation in the woods, visualize the trees, the branches and trunks, the colors of the leaves and the contrast of the blue sky with the white billowing clouds gently drifting by. Smell the aroma of the mossy ground and the damp leaves, the refreshing breeze on your face or the life-sustaining sun warming your body. Remember the fragrance of freshly brewed coffee and breakfast as it is being prepared over the open campfire.

Applying the same principle to the scene of your own home, you may visualize yourself sitting down preparing for an appetizing breakfast there: smelling the freshly baked cinnamon rolls and the fragrance of freshly brewed coffee. Behold your platter of bacon, eggs and toast sitting upon a newly pressed white tablecloth. At the far side of the table sits a large jar of bright red strawberry jam. In one hand you are holding a slice of warm buttered toast, while in your other hand you extend a clean shinning butter knife across the table to lift a large glob of that shimmering red jam on the blade of your knife. As you carefully draw the knife back towards the toast you see that large beautiful glob of red jam slide off the knife and plop down atop that clean white tablecloth. Can you visualize this scenario? If so, you and your imagination are off to a good start.

Some people do experience difficulties when trying to formulate visual images. A former student of mine, who was shy, introverted, and exhibited a complete lack of confidence, had enrolled in a self-hypnosis course to overcome fears of a pending medical operation. Her recovery from the operation was successful. Later she confided that self-hypnosis had worked so well with her operation that now she would like to remove her excess weight. She weighed 310 pounds. Satisfactory results were not being manifested and she said that she could not even begin to imagine herself slender. Even as a child she was fat; she was born fat, fat in grade school and fat all through her life. I suggested that she find a picture of a body that she would be satisfied with and make that her image. The photo that she selected was that of a movie starlet in a provocative swimsuit pose. She carried this photo in her purse and looked at it daily, telling herself that the image in the photo was her. This woman, during the following two years, proceeded to lose 180 pounds, without any special diets or exercises, but only the use of her imagination and suggestions. She lost her shyness, gained confidence and returned to college. She would often drop by my classes and when I acknowledged her to the other students; she would very proudly address the self-hypnosis class and relate her success story.

Rozetta Swanson Rush remarks, "Imagination is the image-making functioning of Mind. . . . Imagination or imagining is fundamental to each individual and is the creativity of visibility of Mind. It is the spontaneous action of the unconscious forming itself." Albert Einstein has been quoted as saying, "Imagination is the eye of the Soul." Dr.

John M. Dorsey, in his book *Illness or Allness*, describes imagination as "my learning, thinking, perceiving, sensing, or every mental activity... my imagination, my creative intelligence, always and only the natural biological process of and in my individuality, in precisely the same sense that my breathing is."[2]

References

1. Henry Lee Bolduc, "A Hypnotic Suggestion," *New Age Journal* (Jan-Feb. 1989).
2. Rozella Swanson Rush, *Me, Myself, and I* (Allison Park, PA: Rozella Swanson Rush, 1982), p. 21.

Other readings

Samuels, Michael. *Healing with the Mind's Eye.* New York, NY: Summit Books, 1990.

Selby, John. *Conscious Healing.* New York, NY: Bantam Books, 1989.

Fanning, Patrick. *Visualization for Change.* Oakland, CA: New Harbinger Publications, Inc.,1988.

CHAPTER 10
Belief

"What things soever ye desire, when ye pray believe that ye receive them, and ye shall have them." ~ Mark 11:24

It is paramount to state—I believe. Stop and ponder, specifically, just what do you believe?

Belief is based on:
1. Your personal experience
2. Your acceptance from an authority figure
3. Your acceptance of faith (religious beliefs)

How much of what we believe is an actual fact, a piece of fiction, or a falsehood that we accept? Fact is the truth as we currently view the situation, but facts change with the passing of time. It was, in the past, a fact among most scholars that the world was flat because scientifically, it was reasoned that if it were round, people would fall off the bottom. In the early 1900s much of the scientific world scoffed at the Wright Brothers' attempts to fly and made disparaging remarks like, "If God wanted man to fly then mankind would have been born with wings." Compare this earlier reasoning to the advancement of today's super jets. The non-believer has difficulty in accepting thoughts and ideas that are either new or in conflict with prior accepted notions.

Science has not entirely discovered the makeup or method of how the human mind functions. We cannot even prove the actual existence of the mind; yet everyone appears to believe that they have a mind and a very good one.

If self-hypnosis is to be important to you, it is imperative to program yourself into believing that you can do it and thereby become successful. **But first you must develop confidence and belief in yourself.**

This is the case history of Sam W, a burly overweight negative-minded 56-year-old male employed as a welder, who was attending my self-hypnosis class at Community College. His negative attitude at times was disruptive to the normal harmony of the class. Sam's normal response was "I don't believe it" or "I can't buy that."

One class session involved discussion of the Belief Factor in self-hypnosis. I emphasized the importance of thinking and believing that your desired outcome would occur, and that one should ignore the situation that you wished to avoid. Sam merely shook his head with his usual non-believing scowl on his face. I used the illustration that if you touch a hot object, immediately tell yourself that "it's cool."

The following week Sam walked into the classroom, beaming all over. He announced to the class that he had to relate his recent experience. He said, "Yesterday I picked up a heavy piece of metal, with my bare hands that another welder had been working on. It was sizzling hot. I told myself that my hands were cool and I placed the metal back on the welding table. My hands were cool—and I did not get burned."

Sam displayed his hands, which normally should have been covered with blisters. They were clean and had absolutely no sign of discoloration or skin damage. Sam looked at me and said, "Norb, up until yesterday I didn't believe any of the stuff you were telling us, but now I am totally convinced."

Sam followed up his newfound belief by going on a self-imposed weight loss program. In the next seven days he lost six pounds with his ultimate goal of taking off another sixty. He told the class that if he could control the pain and burning process then **he believed that he could accomplish anything.**

Dr. E. Arthur Winkler, founder of St. John's University, in his book *God Wants You Healthy,* reminds us:

> We sometimes think of mental healing as if it is a fairly recent idea. However, as far back as recorded history goes, we find that mental healing, under various names and different techniques, has been practiced with apparent success.
>
> In the oldest civilization with which we are acquainted, in Egypt, hundreds of years before the appearance of Jesus, mental healing had a prominent place. There is evidence that the priests had developed techniques for stimulating the human mind to produce amazing healings. In those remote ages, it was believed to be "a gift of the gods."

Excavations at Cavvadias furnished a myriad of interesting material, showing that the miraculous cures of Epidarus were produced at that ancient Greek shrine by suggestion, and in the same manner today, at Lourdes.

Livy tells us that the temples of the gods of Rome were rich in the number of offerings that people gave in return for the cures they received. And Pliny tells of Etruscan spells used by Theophrastus for sciatica, by Cato for the cure of dislocated limbs, and by Varro for gout.

In those early days the power was attributed directly to the gods, However, psychologists today have found answers that reveal it was accomplished in accordance with the laws of nature. Whether the healing takes place at some shrine, or by touching some holy relic, or through the laying on of hands by a healing evangelist, or through hypnosis, or by the denial of the disease by Christian Science; it is the power of the mind over the body working through the law of suggestion.[1]

Belief can create miracles, as in the case history of Peter, (male 60 years old), an internationally renowned ballet dancer, who was teaching ballet with a local ballet company. Peter was involved in an auto accident that resulted in a crushed hip and fractured femur. Immediately after the operation on a Monday morning, the physician stated in the prognosis, "It will take a miracle if you will ever be able to walk again." Peter was devastated. Without the ability to dance he did not have desire to live.

The following day Peter telephoned a distant friend, and informed her of his intent to terminate his life. She remembered that Peter had previously seen me for self-hypnosis. She called me and disclosed that Peter was saving all of the pain killers, his sedative pills, and was determined to take a massive dose and thereby terminate his existence.

I immediately rescheduled my Wednesday evening appointments and visited Peter. He apparently was not aware that his friend had contacted me. During the visit I offered him a relaxation and healing session, which he readily accepted. My suggestions were directed to the easing of his discomfort, rapid healing and a few brief statements regarding the value of life. I reiterated that with his BELIEF and the power of his subconscious mind, he would soon be back teaching ballet.

The miracle that the physician referred to happened that night. When the doctor examined Peter on his Thursday morning rounds (three days after the operation), Peter, in a body cast that extended from his left knee to over his waist, swung himself over the side of the bed and pushed himself to an upright position. Placing all his weight on his left leg (the recently operated side) Peter struck a ballet pose. Needless to say, the doctor was absolutely dumbfounded. Peter walked out of the hospital ten days later and returned to his dancing profession.

When I heard of Peter standing, I was probably more shocked than the physician. I did not at any time give him such a foolhardy idea—but apparently his subconscious mind overrode my suggestions and the miracle materialized. **The power of belief is paramount.**

Dan Custer emphasizes the power of belief in *The Miracle of Mind Power*, as he wrote:

> Knowing I have the intelligence and the power I can say, I WILL, I *am*! Therefore, I *can*! And, therefore, I *will*! Whenever we are confronted with a problem, big or little, we can take these three mental steps. *I am; I can; I will*. When we accept this concept without reservation, we find the situation which faces us is not an obstacle. It is rather a challenge to our power and to our recognition of who and what we are.
>
> One of the greatest evils in human experience is a feeling of weakness and inadequacy—the fear to go ahead because of a belief that we do not have the proper equipment to meet the challenges before us. When we finally recognize ourselves as incarnations of infinite Life using the infinite, creative mind; when we open the channels of our consciousness to infinite intelligence, power and guidance, we literally may become "supermen." To some extent every person can experience this.
>
> I have seen people's lives completely changed through an understanding and continued use of this one simple statement—*I am, I can, and I will*.
>
> *Knowing the truth about yourself, applying the truth you know to yourself and beginning to express that truth in your every action, you can change your whole outlook and experience*. When you do this, you will be using the intelligence and power of universal, creative mind which is all the intelligence and power there is. There is no power to oppose it, ***I am; I can; I will!***[2]

The late hypnotist Douglas Teeple, author of *The Artist Within*, wrote:

> What we are and what we become are a result of our thinking, and any action, whether good or bad, can be described as a precipitated and manifested thought. No action that is single and voluntary may be performed without the motion of the mind, no matter how instantaneous and simple the thought may seem. From each action of the mind, the lifting of an arm, the moving of a finger, the raising of a foot, rising from or sitting in a chair—each act, each motion, exists as a thought in the mind before the thought appears as an act manifest. Our physical welfare and being is therefore the outcome of our thoughts and depends upon which thoughts and actions have been decided upon in the past. Thought, therefore, decides not only what we do but what we are as well, showing in a true form why we should sift out negative and undesirable thoughts and change them into a higher vibratory force.[3]

References

1. Arthur E. Winkler, *God Wants you Healthy* (Springfield, LA: St. John's Publications, 1993), pp. 59-60.
2. Dan Custer, *The Miracle of Mind Power* (Glendale, CA: Westwood Publishing Co., 1960), pp. 248-249.
3. Douglas M. Teeple, *The Artist Within* (New York, NY: Exposition Press, 1965), p. 16.

CHAPTER 11
Suggestions

"Nurture your mind with good thoughts, to believe in the heroic makes heroes." ~Disraeli

The success or failure of self-hypnosis is manifested by the types of suggestions that are programmed into the subconscious mind. Your mind always reacts in a direct fashion, as all suggestions will produce direct results. To gain positive results, the individual must meticulously screen all thoughts, statements, suggestions and affirmations to assure that all negative words and innuendoes are eliminated. The subconscious mind does not always react to the word alone but rather to the visual interpretation that the word conveys. You would never say "I want to lose this fatty weight." The subconscious would picture the fatty weight and assume that you were sending a picture of wanting to be fat. Your subconscious only registers words that it can imagine or picture. One cannot visualize the words "I want to lose" but the words "fatty weight" immediately produces a definite image. A positive approach would be the suggestion, "I will have a slender body" or, "My body is slender, active and energetic."

The alcoholic who strives to impress his mind that "I don't want any whiskey" or "I want to stop drinking" is really only sending a picture to their subconscious mind of *drinking* or of *whiskey*. Your mind accepts this mental photo and interprets it as you wanting to imbibe, and starts sending that compulsive signal to you, causing you to want a drink.

A far better suggestion to your inner self would be, "I am in control of myself. I am a responsible person in control of my actions. I am a sober, responsible person. I am proud of myself and I will be successful in any endeavor that I may commit myself to." Visualize only the positive results that you wish to attain.

Dr. Abarbanel-Brandt believes that by following these assumptions for the construction of auto-hypnotic suggestions, one can arrive at the following criteria for the formation of the most effectual, least harmful phrases:

I. Hypnotic suggestions need to be permissive, expansive, growth encouraging, non-repressive, and non-prohibitory. They need to suggest movement of change, rather than stasis; and to suggest the process of this change as a means towards the desired end. Grammatically, the verb form of change and continuity, the *-ing* form, should be stressed, and the end desire expressed as a comparative rather than an absolute state. Typical examples include: "I can feel better," "I am feeling better," "My ability to make decisions is improving," "The healing process can go on without hindrance."

II. Hypnotic suggestions need to be truthful, i.e., not in conflict with observed facts. To give an example, suppose that a fifty-year patient wanted to feel younger, and was trying to obtain the younger feeling by auto-suggestion. "He would not say "I am young, I am young." For most the adjective "young" applies to the ages below twenty. It would be better to say "I can feel younger," thus suggesting a condition relative to that of the present.

III. Similarly, hypnotic suggestions need to be given in such a way as to minimize possibility of failure. The person who attempts to alleviate a headache by means of auto-suggestion should *not* say "When I open my eyes my headache will be gone" until he has had sufficient practice with voluntary control of the so-called involuntary functions, the chances are that a considerable length of time will ensue before the head pain will (or can) diminish. If the person sets up a rigid, arbitrary time for the attaining of his suggestions, he is increasing the probability of failure of the technique and subsequent disappointment.

It would be better, therefore, to suggest a process of relative improvement, to use the phrasing "My head is feeling more and more comfortable." The less practiced person who might otherwise fail at the more ambitious undertaking is far more likely to have some modest success in the less rigid (less absolute, more relative) situation. This modest success would encourage further effort and relative improvement in succeeding of continuous attempts.

IV. Hypnotic suggestions need not be phrased is such a way as NOT to suggest the condition which one is trying to eliminate. For example the patient with the headache should NOT say "My headache is getting better." This phrase can mean literally "I am getting a better headache." In this context "better" might stand for "larger," "more obvious," "more desirable," "more effective," etc.

The phrase thus announces that a headache exists, and then ameliorates the existence of the pain. It has been pointed out elsewhere that the hypnotist must learn to vocalize his suggestions in positive terms, to lay stress on the desired idea rather than on the idea one wishes to eliminate, which would only mean concentrating on the pain and on the feeling of distress, whereas one should be conveying to the subconscious the idea of the feeling of well-being that one desires.

V. Hypnotic suggestions need to be unequivocal. A typical example of the equivocal suggestion is the statement "I want to get better." In this context the word "want" is assumed to mean "desire." "Want," however, is a verbal symbol for another aspect of human activity; it is equisignificant to "lack" or "I do not have." The statement "I want to get better" might also mean—"I have a deficiency of getting-betterness."—

There are many other words which can possibly set up an equivocal state: wish, hope, need, must, should, ought, have to, got to, like to. All of these seem to imply that the person is directing his energies to "needing" or being compelled, rather than to self-chosen and satisfying action. "Try," moreover, is also a word labeling the unsuccessful attempt. We often hear children use the excuse "I tried to, but couldn't do it." The child gets credit for having tried, but in this case he is also being acknowledged as having failed.[1]

Charles Tebbetts, author of SELF-HYPNOSIS and other mind expanding techniques, suggests that in structuring your suggestions, practice the following principles.

1. *The motivating desire must be strong.* Before you start to write your suggestions, choose a reason or a number of reasons why you want your suggestion carried out. This must be a counter-emotional motivator to replace the behavior pattern you are intending to eliminate. If you are overeating, your present emotional motivator may be the enjoyment you derive from tasting certain foods. The emotions that might be chosen to replace this habit could be a desire for better health, a pretty figure, looking better in clothes, or becoming more attractive to some particular person you care for.
2. *Be positive.* If you say "I will stop eating too much" you are REMINDING the subconscious mind that you eat too much, thereby suggesting the very idea you want to eliminate. If you say "My headache will be gone when I come out of hypnosis" you are suggesting a headache. To frame these thoughts positively, you should say, "I am always

well satisfied with a small meal, I enjoy eating only at meal times, and after I have eaten food amounting to approximately four hundred calories, I push my plate away and say that's enough. I get up from the table feeling entirely satisfied and enjoy the resulting loss of weight." If you wish to suggest that your headache will go away you should say "My head feels better and better. It is clear and relaxed. My head feels good. It will continue to feel good after I come out of hypnosis, because all of the nerves and muscles are rested, relaxed and normal." **Never mention the negative idea you intend to eliminate**. Repeat and emphasize the positive idea you are replacing it with.

3. *Always use the present tense.* Never say "Tomorrow I will feel good" but rather "Tomorrow I feel good."
4. *Set a time limit.* Remember, your subconscious mind is a goal-striving mechanism, and once programmed toward a goal it never stops until it achieves it. Set a realistic time limit, and you will find that the goal is usually reached well before the time you set!
5. *Suggest action, not ability to act.* Don't say, "I have the ability to dance well" but rather " I dance well, with ease and grace."
6. *Be specific.* Choose a self-improvement suggestion you are anxious to carry out, and work with that one suggestion until it is accepted. While learning, it is best to start with suggestions that are easier to carry out so that you can see more immediate results.

7. *Keep your language simple.* Speak as though your subconscious were a bright ten-year-old. Use words the average ten-year-old would understand.
8. *Exaggerate and emotionalize.* Remember, your subconscious mind is the seat of the emotions, and exciting, powerful words will influence it. Use descriptive words such as wonderful, beautiful, exciting, great, thrilling, joyous, gorgeous, and tremendous! Say or think these words with feeling.
9. *Use repetition.* When writing your suggestion, repeat it, enlarge upon it, and repeat it again in different words. Embellish it with convincing adjectives — The more often you are exposed to an idea, the more it influences you. — THE BRAIN WILL ALWAYS SEND OUT A MESSAGE TO ACT UPON ANY SUGGESTION, UNLESS CONFLICTING SUGGESTIONS INHIBIT IT. That all forces act along the line of least resistance is a fundamental law of matter. This is also a law of mind, since mind is merely the activity of matter — the result of stimulating nerve cells. The oftener a card is creased, the more likely it is to bend in the same place again. And the oftener a suggestion is acted upon by the UNCRITICAL MIND, the more certain the suggested response is to repeat itself.[2]

Variations of words are largely successful because of the subconscious mind's susceptibility to accept certain "pet" or key verbalisms. Negative words are barbs which tend to weaken the effectiveness of one's suggestions.

References

1. Albert Abarbamel-Brandt, "Semantics of Auto-Suggestion," *The British Journal of Medical Hypnotism*, Vol. 16, No. 4 (1965).
2. Charles Tebbitts, *Self-Hypnosis and Other Mind Expanding Techniques* (Glendale, CA: Westwood Publishing Co., 1977), pp. 42-48.

Other readings

Santanelli. *The Laws of Suggestion*. Columbus, OH: Pyramid Press, 1902.

Winkler, Arthur E. *The Power of Suggestion*. Springfield, LA: St. John's University Publications, 1989.

Long, Max Freedom. *Self-Suggestion*. Ann Arbor, MI: Edward Brothers, Inc. 1958.

CHAPTER 12
The Indispensable Audio CD Recorder

"How wonderful is the human voice! – It is indeed the organ of the Soul. The intellect of man sits enthroned, visibly, on his forehead and in his eye. And when the heart of man is written in his countenance, but the soul reveals itself in the voice only." ~ Longfellow

"To record or not to record that is the question. While many hypno-therapists prefer to work without a recording, I believe that the audio recording device is a very important tool and is invaluable to the effectiveness of self-hypnosis.

Henry Bolduc writes:

> You don't have to go to a hypnotist to open your mind to hypnotic suggestion. With the use of a self-help recording, you can take more control of your own mind and gear it toward accomplishing your objectives. These recordings can help build your mind and remodel your life the way you want it to be. They can help you develop mental strength and put the "self"

back into self-help. You can use your free will to choose what you are going to plant—and reap—in your own mind.

Commercial audio programs are fine for the beginner. But in order to further explore hypnosis, it is better for you to make your own personalized recording. You can achieve greater success by doing this because you will be learning the self-hypnosis process and because you will be programming your audio program to your own specific needs. Recording your own audio can take less than an hour.[1]

Due to the incredible advancements in technology in recent years, creating a quality self-hypnosis recording is easier than ever. Self-hypnosis recordings tend to be very effective when you are working to hasten the learning of self-hypnosis.

Memorizing and repeating affirmations to oneself while attempting to enter that blissful state of hypnosis can be distracting and could ultimately prove to be counterproductive. Therefore, allow yourself to lie back, relax, and listen to your own voice giving you those beneficial positive suggestions.

Many people resent suggestions or being told what to do by others. They are more responsive to their own ideas, advice and suggestions. By recording your own prepared session and listening to it while in self-hypnosis, you are feeding back into your subconscious mind those suggestions you genuinely wish to accept.

Technology makes it easy to create a quality recording through a variety of different vehicles.

The most effective way to create your recording is by turning your home computer into a recording studio. All that is required to produce a basic audio on your computer is a microphone and recording software. Prices on these vary greatly however, both items are available to meet anybody's budget. If you own an Apple computer then you already have recording software preinstalled on your computer. Using a computer makes it easy to edit your recordings, easily add music, and turn into a CD.

If you don't have access to a computer the next best option is to use a digital voice recorder, or DVR. DVR's are much more reliable than in the past and can now produce clear recordings. Also, they no longer require tapes and most models can store several hours of audio. DVR's allow you to record many self-hypnosis sessions and take them with you anywhere you go.

You can also create self-hypnosis recordings now on your cell phone. The new smart phones such as the iPhone now have applications available for download that give you the ability to make voice recordings right on your phone. Some of these applications can even be downloaded for free.

The major advantage of recording your own self-hypnosis session is that you can preview your results, edit your suggestions to ensure the elimination of negative input, and if necessary, re-record your suggestive words until you have completed an audio program that is satisfactory to your requirements.

The inclusion of background music is optional, provided the music does not remind you of past experiences. It should be low, soothing, relaxing, and without lyrics, thereby enhancing the quality and effectiveness of your tape. Music will also maintain a sense of continuity, by filling possible voids that may occur between suggestions. There are many background relaxation CDs available on the market with almost any mood you may prefer—the ocean, countryside, a babbling brook, perhaps a heavy rainfall.

Prepare a list (of moderate length) of the suggestions you wish to imprint into your subconscious. Review the wording to eliminate negative connotations; remember that phrasing such as "I don't want a cigarette" will send the visual input of a cigarette, and your subconscious mind will interpret that thought as—you wanting a cigarette. If you say, "I want to lose this fat" your subconscious mind visualizes a fat body and believes that you want a fat body. Your subconscious mind will do all within its power to fulfill what it believes you desire.

When you are satisfied with your script and the background music, select a quiet room free of distracting noises. Make yourself comfortable and speak into the microphone. Refer to yourself as YOU—never "I." If you were listening to a recording where the voice kept repeating, "I will do" this or that, you would reject the suggestions because you could care less what some other "I" would say. Give appropriate verbalisms to yourself in this manner. You are now ready to relax and accept the suggestions that you desire to effect changes in your attitude, health, or abilities. Your suggestions should be repeated several times, but each time you repeat the thought, change the wording. For example: "Your eyes are becoming tired," "Your eyes are sagging," "The eyelids are drooping," etc. Repetitious wording such as "You are getting sleepy, you are getting sleepy, you are getting sleepy," has a tendency to irritate and aggravate the individual and inadvertently produce less than satisfactory results.

Henry Bolduc states that the steps necessary for making your self-help audio program are as simple as the A-B-Cs.

> STEP A. Begin your recording with suggestions designed to guide *you into self-hypnosis.* Some people call this stage "achieving alpha," others call it "centering." This chapter contains two separate methods for "Entering Self-Hypnosis," (1) a traditional, direct approach and (2) a naturalistic style approach. In time you can design your own method — or combine favorite parts of both approaches — for entering self-hypnosis.
>
> STEP B. Continue your recording with *cycles of positive suggestions and creative visualization exercises.* Here is where you plant the seeds of tomorrow's bountiful harvest, where you are building your new reality — creating your own miracles.
>
> STEP C. Complete your recording with an *"emerging"* procedure. Some people call this "returning to everyday awareness" or "coming back to beta level." At this point you may insert suggestions for automatically going into regular nighttime sleep.[2]

Bolduc defines the traditional method as the progressive relaxation method directed to physical being, while the naturalistic approach is one directed toward mental visualization of relaxation.

In the book *Program Your Own Life* Michael H. Green strongly advocates the use of making recordings. The book offers many self-hypnosis suggestions and scripts that can be incorporated into your tape or CD.

You should spend a substantial amount of time in preparing your audio script. It should not be done hastily. In fact, it should be done only after you have worked for some time with your suggestion and your imagery. I recommend that you work one week with the suggestion alone, another week with the imagery and the suggestion combined, and during that two-week period of time write and rewrite your audio script until you have it exactly the way you want it. The reason you should be so methodical about the preparation of this audio script is that once you play this tape for approximately three weeks you can count on it being in your unconscious for the rest of your life. You can see how important it is to make sure you have precisely what you want well prepared in advance.[3]

To write out your desired goal and the expectation of positive results in your specialized script may be an enjoyable challenge. If this seems difficult and you are not convinced that you have the ability to prepare a constructive dialog, I would recommend that you secure professionally prepared scripts. Michael Greene has written *Program Your Own Life* to offer prepared scripts both to the beginner in self-hypnosis and the professional hypnotherapist.[4] Dr. Arthur Winkler has written over 500 scripts to be used by hypnotherapists. These are available in two volumes and written in a manner that the hypnotist or self-hypnotist could either read them directly, or utilize the information in the preparation of their own scripts.[5] Ronald Havens and Catherine Walters have published *Hypnotherapy Scripts*, with scripts based on Erickson's techniques.[6] Another recommended script book is *Creative Scripts for Hypnotherapy*, printed in 1994 and written by Marlene E. Hunter.[7]

References

1. Henry Bolduc, "A Hypnotic Suggestion," *New Age Journal* (Jan-Feb. 1989).
2. Ibid., *Self-Hypnosis: Creating Your Own Destiny* (Virginia Beach, VA: A.R.E. Press, 1985), p. 59.
3. Michael H. Greene, *Program Your Own Life* (Marshall, VA: Behavioral Systems Inc., 1982), p. 33.
4. Ibid.
5. Arthur Winkler, *Hypnotic Prescriptions, Vols. I & II* (Springfield, LA: St. John's Publications, 1991 & 1993).
6. Ronald Havens & Catherine Walters, *Hypnotherapy Scripts* (New York, NY: Brunner/Mazel, 1989).
7. Marlene Hunter, *Creative Scripts for Hypnotherapy* (New York, NY: Brunner/Mazel, 1994).

CHAPTER 13
Other Routes to Self-Hypnosis

"Everything can be taken from a man but one thing: The last of human freedoms – to choose one's attitude in any given set of circumstances, to choose one's own way." ~ Victor Frankl

The pathway to successful self-hypnosis varies with each individual. The self-directed, self-proficient can-do person may achieve the desired result by reading about the subject and then, with the required dedication, applying the principles and rules outlined here. The "Forty Count Method" of achieving self-hypnosis has proven to be successful to thousands of dedicated aspirants. Maintain the acronym of C.R.I.B.S. Some may succeed in short-cutting these essential ingredients, but your chances for success become multiplied when you apply COMMITMENT, RELAXATION, IMAGERY, BELIEF, and SUGGESTIONS as a vital part of your program.

The insecure person, or one without initiative, may require several sessions with a qualified hypnotist to learn, experience and feel the sensations of hypnotic trance. Many authors of hypnotism and self-hypnosis books believe that the best or only way to achieve ultimate results with hypnosis is to approach it under the direction of a hypnotist. You will be hypnotized several times and implanted with the suggestions that whenever you perform a certain act or recite specific cue words, you will automatically go into that prearranged self-hypnosis state. This premise I cannot accept. A person that is reacting to a post-hypnotic suggestion is still responding to the hypnotist and is not entirely in a pure self-hypnotic state.

Erica Fromm and Stephen Kahn, co-authors of *Self Hypnosis: the Chicago Paradigm*, define self-hypnosis as follows:

> In stringently defined self-hypnosis, which we call "hypnotist-absent self-hypnosis," no hypnotist is present. In more loosely defined self-hypnosis, to be called "hypnotist-present self-hypnosis," the hypnotist may still be present, but the usual hetero-hypnotic verbal and nonverbal interactions have been altered. For example, an hypnotist present during self-hypnosis may remain silent, he may speak to the subject but indicate through his inflections that the words are not intended to be suggestions, or he may give suggestions in a modified or reduced form.
>
> Historically, clinicians and researchers alike have come to varying views on the relative utility of the hypnotist's presence during self-hypnosis. To many clinicians, a patient is considered to engage in self-hypnosis when she practices hypnotic techniques alone, outside the clinical hour, although these techniques have been taught to the patient by the hypnotist/clinician.[1]

Starting a self-help self-hypnosis group is a method highly recommended by Henry Bolduc. The group could explore the possibilities of exchanging ideas on the effectiveness of their own self-hypnosis tapes. He recommends that the group study Edgar Cayce readings on "Suggested Therapeutics" and "Visualization and Mind! The Builder," and also books about Milton Erickson. The members of the self-help group should incorporate what they have learned from Erickson and Cayce into their own self-help programming tapes.

Bolduc recommends that you take classes in hypnotism, but for general self-help all you need are high ideals and a sincere desire for personal improvement.

The most exciting and inexpensive way to learn hypnosis is to start a self-help study group as:
1. A small group of two or three working together is far more influential than two or three dozen working alone.
2. The group could have a different moderator at each meeting. Study traditional areas of hypnosis, or innovative new methods — like making tapes. This is a "learn as you study and share" type of approach.
3. As an established group you could invite guest speakers.
4. As you and your group begin to realize that you have self educated yourselves in a personal and profound manner your action will reach out and inspire others. Helping others to help themselves. You have drawn out what was al-

ready there deep within yourself, and having brought it out you've shared your light with others.

Your study group may not enlighten the entire planet, but it will bring light to illuminate your own area. It is said that if you wish to plant for days, plant flowers: if you wish to plant for years, plant trees: but if you wish to plant for eternity, plant ideas.[2]

References

1. Erica Fromm & Stephen Kahn, *Self-Hypnosis: the Chicago Paradigm* (New York, NY: Guilford Press, 1990), p. 45.
2. Henry L. Bouduc, "Starting a Self Help Program," *NewRealities* (Jan-Feb. 1990).

CHAPTER 14
Sensible Precautions

"Take warning by the misfortunes of others, that others may not example from you." ~ Saadi

For years the general public has been negatively influenced by the motion picture industry's negative portrayal of hypnosis and the evils performed under the **spell** of hypnosis. Mr. John Q. Public believes that the hypnotist has unlimited powers and can cause a person, when placed in an hypnotic trance, to perform or commit any act the hypnotist commands. This conception is false, inaccurate, and grossly misleading.

An unethical hypnotist could, over a period of time, brainwash or program a subject to perform unethical, immoral, or anti-social acts. So too, could any salesman, lawyer, counselor, doctor, clergyman, or anyone who advises, advocates, teaches, or even suggests words of evil intent. In dealing with people, we must not allow our minds to accept negative suggestions, but simply place our confidence in our God-given intelligence and in those individuals who are worthy of our trust.

In discussing the possible dangers of self-hypnosis, Dr. Kroger writes:

> Auto-hypnosis in one ritualistic form or another, is employed in Zen Buddhist Meditation, the Samadhic state of Yoga, the Jewish Cabalistic state of Kavannah and various other religious rites. The hypnotic relationship and auto-hypnosis, even though denied, are also responsible for the recoveries obtained by Christian Science, Science of Mind, Theosophy, the Emmanuel Movement, and many other spiritualistic religious modalities. Therefore it is difficult to see how auto-hypnosis can be dangerous when the very essence of prayer is based on the fundamental principles of auto-hypnosis.[1]

Many people have the desire to learn self-hypnosis to control, minimize, or eliminate pain. This is acceptable, but only when the cause of the discomfort has been learned, or is being treated by a physician. Never, under any circumstances, alleviate pain with self-hypnosis just to mask the symptoms. Many wish to bury their heads, like the proverbial ostrich, believing that anything serious will pass away. One might think, for example, that a migraine could be a result of a little tension, when actually it may prove to be fatal, for that supposed migraine could instead be an aneurysm or an early development of a brain tumor, among many possibilities.

If you have a problem, or suspect that you may harbor a medical disorder, consult your doctor. The medical world has diagnostic equipment with which to pinpoint a potential medical condition. Your skill with self-hypnosis can then be applied and put to good use by controlling the discomfort and promoting faster healing.

A seemingly well-qualified hypnotist, highly respected in the healing arts, boasted that he possessed the ability to control an excruciating pain he had been experiencing for the past four years. He had never visited a medical doctor, nor did he have the slightest notion what caused his pain; but under self-hypnosis he continued to block out the discomfort mentally. One day when he could no longer stand erect, the man was promptly admitted to a local hospital. There X-rays revealed he had bone cancer throughout his entire upper leg. The limb was later amputated. Unfortunately the cancer had metastasized and spread throughout his entire body. By then it was too late and consequently he died. Had the man followed common sense procedures and checked with the appropriate medical experts a few years earlier, perhaps the cancer could have been arrested, contained, removed, or cured and this man would be alive today.

Be intelligent and use self-hypnosis in a prudent manner. Do not become a statistic because of your refusal to accept medical assistance. Medical science has diagnostic equipment that has progressed to the state of a technical art, and it is advancing more each day.

WARNING: THE SCIENCE OF SELF-HYPNOSIS can serve as a means of effective alternative medical treatment but it should be considered as complementary to proper medical diagnosis and subsequent care. Do not, under any circumstance, employ self-hypnosis to remove or mask pain or any other symptoms that may be a warning sign or signal of a serious medical complication.

Never be concerned about losing control:

> Volitional control is never lost in the self-hypnosis trance state. If self-control is lost it is no longer self-hypnosis, for the individual drifts into a deeper trance which immediately turns into ordinary sleep from which he will wake in a normal manner. The length of time he sleeps will depend on how tired and comfortable he is, what external distractions are happening and what waking suggestions he has made to himself before beginning the suggestions session.[2]

Eliminate negative thoughts and learn, whenever possible, to convert those negative suggestions into positive constructive actions. In our world of unlimited potential and abundance, we are constantly bombarded with negative suggestions. It has been estimated that between 90 and 95 percent of the nation's people are basically negative in their attitudes. The majority of people believe that they cannot possibly succeed academically or in business and are unable to influence their own health and attitudes. Negativity may be compared to weeds growing in a flower garden. Tender care, proper feeding, cultivation, watering, and weeding are required to achieve the best flowers and to keep them healthy. Weeds seem to persist and grow profusely under all conditions, requiring constant work to eliminate or keep under control. Even after the most stringent care, sometimes seeds and portions of the root structure remain behind to keep the nuisance weeds alive.

Negative thoughts, as well, must be removed—stems, roots, and seeds. Self-hypnosis can help recognize and eliminate the negative "weeds" and direct our efforts towards a more positive attitude and healthy fulfillment of life.

Beware of any hypnotist who would advise you *to not* consult with a physician. Ethical hypnotherapists will not teach self-hypnosis nor employ the science of hypnotherapy to address medical problems, without the permission or consent of the client's physician. *A good hypnotherapist prefers to work with the medical profession, not against it!*

Beware of those false hypnotists and hypnotherapists who abound amongst us with legal but often worthless diplomas hanging upon their office walls. Unfortunately, most states in the US do not have an intelligent and properly coordinated regulation system which establishes educational, training, and testing programs before one can apply for the title of HYPNOTHERAPIST or HYPNOTIST. Sadly, with this dire lack of understanding and appropriate legislation, many unqualified and unscrupulous individuals are masquerading as CERTIFIED HYPNOTHERAPISTS.

Your hypnotist may have a wall blanketed with certificates, most of which is just "wall covering" that anyone can purchase for a nominal fee, ranging between 15 to 150 dollars. Certain so-called prestigious hypnosis organizations are guilty of the appalling practice of simply selling their certifications. It is within the realm of possibility for a "hypnotist" to display a wall covered with this wallpaper, never having received a minute of technical hypnotic training. There are unscrupulous so-called trainers certifying people to become HYPNOTISTS with as little as 4, 8 or 12 hours of questionable training. Still others will certify trainees by offering home-study lessons, for listening to a few audio tapes or, perhaps, by purchasing a home-study video course. The sole criteria appears to be, "If your check clears the bank—you qualify."

Titles following a person's name may impress the gullible, but specifically what does that title indicate that would attest to the actual qualification that person may have attained in the art of hypnotism? How could a person with an MD, PhD, DD, DL, MSW, or RN degree be considered qualified to practice hypnosis, without the appropriate training? Many knowledgeable instructors without a professional degree have taught hundreds of medical doctors, dentists, psychologists, chiropractors, and clergymen the science and practice of hypnotism. Some of these truly qualified hypnotists in the edification of hypnosis are Dewey Deavers, Robert Bellus, Dave Elman, Gil Boyne, and Charles Tebbitts.

Beware, while you are studying self-hypnosis, that the self-hypnosis that you are learning is for YOU. This learning does not qualify you to become a hypnotist. One of my clients used hypnosis for her forthcoming childbirth. The results were impressive and her husband was so intrigued that he enrolled in a self-hypnosis class that I was teaching. After a few sessions he proceeded to hypnotize his wife who was a deep trancer and willing subject. The induction was successful but when he attempted to bring her out of the hypnotic state, she refused. He panicked and his further attempts only aggravated the situation. He placed an emergency call to me and I had him hold the phone to his wife's ear while I terminated the trance. Needless to say, he learned a lesson and did not attempt to hypnotize others after that drastic experience.

References

1. William S. Kroger, "It is a wise hypnotist who knows who is hypnotizing whom," *The British Journal of Medical Hypnotism*, Vol. 13, No. 4 (1962).
2. William J. Ousby, *Self-Hypnosis and Scientific Self-Suggestion* (New York, NY: A.R.C. Books Inc., 1969), p. 84.

Other readings

Sadler, William S. *The Mind at Mischief.* New York, NY: Funk & Wagnalls Co., 1929.

Sanders, Shirley. *Clinical Self-Hypnosis.* New York, NY: The Guilford Press, 1991.

CHAPTER 15
Threshold of a New Era

"Thought — self trance, when intelligently harnessed, becomes possessive of multiple and attainable powers which can be found within each of us. MAN, KNOW THYSELF!" ~ Robert A. Bellus

Knowledge of the art of self-trance (self-hypnosis), has been recognized for thousands of traceable years, dating back to the time of the ancient Egyptians. Hypnosis was an acceptable tool of the earliest physicians and was certainly taught in the "medical schools" of the day, which apparently were more advanced in dealing with the mind than we are today.

Fear, produced through superstition as a result of ignorance, and particularly instigated by the teachings of some religious institutions, has all but destroyed our understanding of one of our greatest endowments, the trance (whether self-produced or induced with the assistance of a knowledgeable operator).

In recent years the shell of ignorance surrounding the mysteries of self-hypnosis has been cracked, making available vast amounts of hitherto unrealized information dealing with the human mind and its vital relationship to one's physical brain.

As a result, tens of thousands of well-intentioned people have flocked into the arms of businessmen selling hypnosis lessons. They have been attracted to this cornucopia of erudition, only to discover that their eagerness has led them into the wrong hands, with promises too fanciful to be realized. Meanwhile a true academic-style training program, documented with research and presented through the accepted collegiate community, remains practically nonexistent.

State lawmakers, when confronted with the pros and cons relating to any form of hypnosis, are unable to surface with a sensible answer in the passing of legislation dealing with what has been, up to the present, the "unknown." Too little has been done in the advancement of the science of hypnosis and its related spheres over these thousands of years. But now, all possible questions are expected to be answered almost instantaneously by everyone concerned on all levels of professional endeavor.

Of primary importance is the first step, self-understanding. This quickly leads into the successful practice of self-hypnosis, where the REAL YOU can be reached. Easy? Of course it is. But people, for reasons of their own, complicate even the most simple of sciences.

It must be remembered that we can survive without many of our body organs, but we cannot live without our mind. Therefore it is only logical that our strongest mental ally, the mind, be allotted greater recognition, especially since it is only recently becoming harnessed before the eyes of the slowly awakening public.

Teachers, doctors, parents and even friends unintentionally induce trance states in each other daily in the guise of suggestion; but who effectively advises the casual human to rearrange their own thinking for their own benefit? Many great people can attest to the benefits of self-trance, including a former mayor who, in his younger days, seated himself in an empty mayor's chair and remarked, "One day, I will be sitting in this chair as mayor." His friends laughed then, but within a decade, this man's words came true.

On the foreseeable horizon, the world of hypnotism, and especially the area of self-hypnosis, will emerge from its cocoon-like dormancy and become recognized as an accepted and normal way of life. This realistic prediction will affect and greatly enhance almost every conceivable business, profession, academic study, trade and occupation, and physical sport, and will certainly extend itself into the private matter of sensible, superior sex achievement and for a better and more sustainable family life. Yet, this brief scenario is no more than the tip of the proverbial iceberg.

As intelligence may differ greatly between individuals, it is imperative that we learn to self-hypnotize to enhance our natural talents. It has been said that "hypnosis (in any form) is a tool of psychology," but the reverse can also be true.

The future greatness of the world will be increased to a marked degree by the recognition and deployment of self-hypnosis. With full employment of our natural endowments, brought about through careful planning, prospects for an unparalleled utopian civilization can become sound reality.

Alman and Lambrou, authors of *Self-Hypnosis*, predict an ever-expanding acceptance and utilization of self-hypnosis:

In the near future, Fortune 500 companies will incorporate self-hypnosis training to reduce stress related cardiovascular disease in senior-management. These companies will also institute self-hypnosis to reduce stress-related illnesses and improve productivity.

Another possible application would be for major league baseball teams to use self-hypnosis in spring training camps and can become reality when all players attend daily exercises on relaxation, concentration, and mental rehearsal for greater skill attainment.

Within the range of possibility is the acceptance of self-hypnosis by health insurance companies, with coverage supporting training in self-hypnosis as an adjunct to medical treatment for inducing the immune system to function at its maximum potential against disease.[1]

The future is here, the time is now. We must awaken to the needs and desires of our inner selves and for the aspirations of newer generations to come. Our mastery of self-hypnosis must grow and continue to expand until its golden potential has improved the quality of life around us and helped to create a new and better world.

References

1. Brian M. Alman & Peter Lambrou, *Self-Hypnosis* (New York, NY: Brunner/Mazel, 1983), pp. 271-273.

BIBLIOGRAPHY

Abarbamel-Brandt, A. "Semantics of Auto-Suggestion." *The British Journal of Medical Hypnotism*. Vol. 16, No. 4 (1965).

Adams, P. *The New Self-Hypnosis*. Hollywood CA: Wilshire Book Co., 1967.

Alman, B. M. & P. Lambrou. *Self-Hypnosis*. New York, NY: Brunner/Maszel Publishers, 1983.

Bailes, F. W. *Your Mind Can Heal You*. New York, NY: Dodd, Mead and Company, 1941.

Benson, H. *The Relaxation Response*. New York, NY: Avon, 1976.

Bernhardt, R. & D. Martin. *Self-Mastery through Self-Hypnosis*. Indianapolis, IN: Bobbs Merrill Co.,1977.

Bernheim, H. *Hypnosis-Suggestion in Psychotherapy*. Hyde Park, NY: University Books, 1964.

Bolduc, H. L. "A Hypnotic Suggestion." *New Age Journal* (Jan-Feb, 1989).

_____*Self-Suggestion: Creating Your Own Destiny*. Virginia Beach, VA: A.R.E. Press, 1985.

Brooks, H. C. *The Practice of Autosuggestion*. New York, NY: Dodd, Mead & Co., 1922.

Cannon, A. *The Power Within*. New York, NY: E.P. Dutton & Co. Inc.,1953.

Chopra, D. *Quantum Healing*. New York, NY: Bantam Books, 1990.

_____*Ageless Body, Timeless Mind* (New York, NY: Harmony Books, 1993.

Couè, E. *My Method*. Garden City, NY: Doubleday Page & Co., 1923.

Cousins, N. *Head First*. New York, NY: E. P. Dutton, 1989.

Custer, D. *The Miracle of Mind Power*. Glendale, CA: Westwood Publishing Co., 1960.

Delgado, J. M. R. *Physical Control of the Mind*. New York, NY: Harper & Row Publishers, 1969.

Dossey, L. *Healing Words*. San Francisco, CA: Harper, 1993.

Edmonston, William E. Jr. *Hypnosis and Relaxation*. New York, NY: John Wiley & Sons, 1981.

Fanning, Patrick. *Visualization for Change*. Oakland, CA: New Harbinger Publishing Co., 1988.

Fromm, E. & S. Kahn, *Self-Hypnosis: the Chicago Paradigm*. New York, NY: Guilford Press, 1990.

Gibson, W. C. *Therapeutic Self-Hypnosis*. New York, NY: Caravelle Books, 1967.

Goldberg, B., ed. *Alternative Medicine*. Payallut, WA: Future Medicine Publishing Co.,1993.

Greene, M. H. *Program Your Own Life*. Marshall, VA: Behavioral Systems Inc., 1982.

Haddock, Frank C. *Power of Will*. Meridan, CT: Pelton Publishing Co., 1918.

Hariman, J. *How to use the Power of Self-Hypnosis*. Wellingborough, Northamptonshire: Thorson's Publishers Limited, 1988.

BIBLIOGRAPHY

Havens, R. & C.Walters, *Hypnotherapy Scripts*. New York, NY: Brunner/Mazel, 1989.

Hunter, M. E. *Scripts for Hypnotherapy*. New York, NY: Brunner/Mazel, 1994.

Hunter, R. C. *The Art of Hypnosis*. Merrimack, NH: National Guild of Hypnotists, 1994.

Jacobson, E. *You Must Relax*. New York, NY: McGraw-Hill Book Co., 1957.

Kirtley, C. *Consumer Guide to Hypnosis*. Merrimack, NH: National Guild of Hypnotists, 1991.

Kroger, W. S. "It is a wise hypnotist who knows who is hypnotizing whom." *The British Journal of Medical Hypnotism*. Vol. 13, No. 4. (1962).

Lewis, H. A. *Self-Hypnosis Dynamics*. Oak Park, MI: Lewis Hypnosis & Training Center, 1962.

Linden, W. *Autogenic Training*. New York, NY: The Guilford Press, 1990.

Long, M. F. *Self-Suggestion*. Ann Arbor, MI: Edward Brothers, Inc., 1958.

Marchetti, A. *Beating the Odds*. Chicago, IL: Contempory Books Inc., 1988.

Masters, R. *How Your Mind Can Keep You Well*. Los Angeles, CA: Foundation of Human Understanding, 1971.

Moyers, B. *Healing and the Mind*. New York, NY: Doubleday, 1993.

Olson, K. G. *Encyclopedia of Alternate Health Care*. New York, NY: Philip Lief Group, Inc., 1989.

Ousby, W. J. *Self-Hypnosis and Scientific Self Suggestion*. New York, NY: A.R.E. Books Inc., 1969.

Pachter, H. M. *Magic into Science.* New York, NY: Henry Schuman, 1951.

Pearsall, P. *Super Immunity: Master Your Emotions and Improve Your Health,* New York, NY: Fawcett Gold Medal Books, 1988

Roon, K. *Karin Roon's New Way to Relax.* New York, NY: Greystone Press, 1961.

Rossi, E.L. *The Psychobiology of Mind-Body Healing.* New York, NY: W. W. Norton & Co., 1986.

Rossi, E. L. & D. B. Cheek, *Mind-Body Therapy.* New York, NY: W.W. Norton & Co., 1986.

Rush, R.S. *Me, Myself and I.* Allison Park, PA: Rozella Swanson Rush, 1982.

Sadler, W. S. *The Mind at Mischief.* New York, NY: Funk & Wagnalls Co., 1929.

Salter, A. *What is Hypnosis.* New York, NY: Farrar, Straus & Co., 1944.

Samuels, M. *Healing With the Mind's Eye.* New York, NY: Bantam Books, 1990.

Sanders, Shirley. *Clinical Self-Hypnosis.* New York, NY: The Guilford Press, 1991.

Santanelli, *The Laws of Suggestion.* Columbus, OH: Pyramid Press, 1902.

Schiffman, M. *Self-Therapy.* Menlo Park, CA: Self Therapy Press, 1967.

Siegel, B. *Love, Medicine & Miracles.* New York, NY: Harper & Row, 1986.

Selby, J. *Conscious Healing.* New York, NY: Bantam Books, 1989.

Soskis, David A. *Teaching Self-Hypnosis.* New York, NY: W. W. Norton & Company, 1986.

Stiles, B. *Mind Power to Success*. New Castle, PA: Stiles Associates, 1983.

Straus, R.A. *Creative Self-Hypnosis*. New York, NY: Prentice Hall Press, 1989.

Tebbetts, C. *Self-Hypnosis and other Mind Expanding Techniques*. Glendale, CA: Westwood Publishing Co., 1977.

_____*Miracles on Demand*. Glendale, CA: Westwod Publishing Co., 1987.

Teeple, D. M. *The Artist Within*. New York, NY: Exposition Press, 1965.

Warrenby, Glenn Van. *Self-Hypnosis and Post-Hypnotic Suggestions*. Los Alamitos, CA: Hwong Publishing Co., 1977.

Williams, J. K. *The Knack of Using Your Subconscious Mind*. Englewood Cliffs, NJ: Prentice Hall Inc., 1952.

Winkler, A. E. *God Wants You Healthy*. Springfield, LA: St. John's Publications, 1993.

_____*The Power of Suggestion*. Springfield, LA: St. John's Publications, 1989.

_____*Hypnotic Prescriptions, Vol. I*. Springfield, LA: St. John's Publications, 1991.

_____*Hypnotic Prescriptions, Vol. II*. Springfield, LA: St. John's Publications, 1993.

CPSIA information can be obtained at www.ICGtesting.com
Printed in the USA
BVOW06s0623110616

451648BV00012B/201/P